Wilhelm Dilthey

Wilhelm Dilthey

Pioneer of the Human Studies

H.P. Rickman
Reader in Philosophy, City University, London

University of California Press
Berkeley Los Angeles London

First published in Great Britain in 1979 by
Paul Elek Limited
54–58 Caledonian Road, London N1 9RN

ISBN 0-520-03879-7

Library of Congress Catalog Card Number: 78-68828

University of California Press, Berkeley and Los Angeles, California
University of California Press, Ltd, London, England

Printed in Great Britain

Contents

Preface

The aim of this book is to introduce readers to a remarkable German thinker who influenced modern thought in many fields from sociology, philosophy and psychology to the history of ideas.

Dilthey's interest spanned all the different human disciplines because he saw them as parts of man's search for self-knowledge, the sole basis, he thought, for social, moral and political choices. Because he felt this self-knowledge was so important, he asked if students of human nature were on the right track and how they could improve the accuracy and practical utility of their disciplines. These questions are with us still, for it is far from self-evident that our social surveys, psychological experiments, economic analyses and philosophic debates help us to solve the urgent problems of our time.

Discussions on the nature, aims and methods of the disciplines concerned with man have recently been enlivened by increasing interaction between Anglo-Saxon and Continental scholarship; so in Britain and in America we have had to meet the challenge of phenomenology and existentialism in sociology and psychology as well as in philosophy. We have also been powerfully affected by the work of the Frankfurt school which stimulated methodological debates as well as providing an ideology for some of our recent student rebels. Dilthey influenced all the thinkers we hear so much about today, Husserl and Heidegger, Max Weber, Adorno, Marcuse and Habermas, yet he is something of a ghost at this intellectual feast and has remained relatively unknown. This needs to be remedied.

In this book I have tried to give a clear and systematic account of Dilthey's most important and original theories rather than trace the development of his ideas and the sources of his inspiration. I have also, where possible, stated his views in terms which will allow today's specialists to recognize the links with their own subject; it is obviously impossible to give details of all the theories he influenced and all the problems on which his thoughts have a bearing. Finally, I have illustrated the quality of Dilthey's writing by quotations mostly from works so far untranslated and, to show the continuity of his thought, I have usually grouped together quotations from different works (rather than trace the argument within a particular work).

In conclusion I should like to express my debt to Professor O.F. Bollnow, Professor Emeritus of Tübingen University and one of the leading Dilthey scholars, who most generously helped me in my first attempts to understand Dilthey and has remained a friend ever since. I should also like to thank Professor F. Rodi of Bochum University who was most helpful in giving me information about, and access to, unpublished material; Professor Gründer who provided personal information and the photograph of Dilthey reproduced on the jacket; and Mrs L. Wittel who gave me access to Dilthey's letters and pointed out those of particular interest.

1

The importance of Dilthey

Why read Dilthey today? Why study the ideas of a nineteenth-century German philosopher some seventy years after his death? One answer to this question, which potential English readers might reasonably ask, is that he is widely recognized as a great philosopher. Characteristic of many testimonies to this effect is the view of the famous Spanish thinker, Ortega y Gasset, who called him 'the most important thinker of the second half of the nineteenth century'[1]—a remarkable claim when one remembers that this was the period of Marx and Freud, of Mill, Nietzsche, Max Weber and William James. More recently a Swiss scholar described him as the Newton of the Human Studies.[2]

Such claims may seem, and indeed be, exaggerated but what is significant and needs explaining is that distinguished thinkers and scholars (many more than those I have quoted) have spoken of Dilthey in superlatives. In the English-speaking world, where he has often been misrepresented and is still underestimated, these extreme claims on his behalf provide a corrective, and challenge us to re-examine his achievements and limitations.

Dilthey's impact on modern thinking is a further reason for studying his work. Once we realize how much he influenced phenomenology and existentialism, the development of the history of ideas, the psychological study of personality and Max Weber's sociology we are encouraged to think that we might understand these new ideas better by going back to their roots.[3] Today, in Britain, there is an increasing interest in continental thought. After a period of mutual suspicion and even contempt, thinkers on both sides of the Channel have begun to realize that they

1

could learn from each other because, in spite of their differences in style and tradition, they share common problems and are even seeking solutions on the same lines. The work of contemporary German philosophers and sociologists is being translated into English and going back to Dilthey can help us to understand it better.

For many people, particularly those interested in the history of ideas, Dilthey's importance and influence may be sufficient reasons for taking an interest in him. Others may think that once a man has exercised his influence his ideas are best enjoyed in the contemporary works into which they have been absorbed (no one doubts Newton's greatness and influence but few physicists read him today). There is, however, a further reason to attract readers to Dilthey and, indeed, account for the fact that he is actively read today—his collected works are being republished and extended, and recently several monographs about him have appeared.[4] This further reason is the most important of all. It shows that Dilthey's ideas have remained directly relevant to the problems of our time. His main claim to attention is that he says things which have not been said, or not said so well, by anyone else. What I think this distinctive and far from out-dated contribution is, I shall try to suggest in this chapter and work out more fully throughout the book. I shall also deal with the supplementary questions which are likely to arise in the readers' minds: why does Dilthey, in spite of his greatness, still need introducing? Why have his thoughts not been fully absorbed, his lessons learned? To answer these questions we shall have to look at the curious history of his writings.

One of the things that, even today, we may need reminding of is the practical importance of philosophy. Dilthey, in conformity with a long tradition dating back to Socrates and Plato, believed that philosophy should provide personal and social guidance. By the beginning of the nineteenth-century this idea had been eroded, partly by the increase in specialization and partly by the fact that most philosophers were by then university teachers (usually in the pay of the state) who thought it unwise, sometimes unsafe, and always immodest, to claim a leading role for philosophy. But Dilthey, like his contemporaries Marx and Nietzsche, felt that philosophy was nothing if it had no bearing on human life. Though as sceptical as many of his contemporaries about the powers of reason to penetrate the ultimate structure of reality and deduce moral principles from it, Dilthey refused to resign himself to irrationalism about moral issues. He was convinced that through empirical research and philosophic reflection man could come to know himself and his history and from this derive principles of action. The only alternative—once we have rejected divine revelation and direct access to a Platonic realm of ideas—namely that knowledge and reason have no bearing on action, he could not accept. Though theoretical, in the sense of being about broad fundamental issues rather than specific ones like devising a new highway code, philosophy was, for him, about living in the practical world. The purpose of theory is practice. 'It is useless', Dilthey wrote as quite a young man, 'to go on sharpening the knife if the wood is there waiting to be carved' (Vol. XVIII, p1).[5]

The philosopher's first job, if he is to be useful, is to diagnose the problems which need to be solved. In one sense these are only too obvious and no philosopher is needed to make us aware of the dangers of inflation or the risk of being mugged at night, but the whole pattern of a civilization of which these problems are parts and symptoms, is not so easily understood; acute, but selective and critical, appreciation of the facts has been considered one of the philosopher's tasks from antiquity to the eighteenth-century, from Plato to Rousseau. Today Marxists and existen-tialists, in particular, still consider this their business but the majority of philosophers have lost their nerve and passed this job on to sociologists and speculative historians who, as a conse-quence, have gained wide popularity among the young. Dilthey's position is poised between a speculative and a factual interpret-ation of society; he appreciated the need for the carefully compiled data provided by the empirical disciplines and for the critical philosophic analysis to which they must be submitted.

The problems which Dilthey diagnosed are still—details apart—ours: the social and political problems of a rapidly chang-ing world, the moral uncertainties of an age without faith, and questions about controlling and organizing increasingly complex societies. Among the features of his age which he noted, in one

3

of his lecture courses,[6] as particularly important were the dominance of science, the decline of religion and metaphysics, and the new realism both in life and literature. He was also very interested in the spread of mass-movements pressing for greater political participation, and was acutely aware of the issues they raised.

What is old [he wrote] cannot just be renewed; loyalty, divine grace, feudal rights of dominion without office, the particular details of Christian religious life, conventional morality and idealistic poetry all belong to the past. We are faced with the task of constructing anew a social order which transfers the valid aspects of individualism to a socially-conceived order of society. Such a task requires the cooperation of philosophy because it can help us to achieve a successful solution. (*Nachlass*, C34, Vol. II, p.156)[7]

I doubt if one can improve on the phrase about transferring 'the valid aspects of individualism to a socially-conceived order of society' as a description of one of the major requirements of our civilization.

In a letter to his friend York[8] (December 1892, *Letters*, p.156)[9] he wrote even more grimly about our problems and pointed to one particular cause.

Catastrophe is approaching us with terrible rapidity; we are being led into it by our lack of faith, incapacity to find, maintain or—which amounts to the same thing—re-create fresh convictions about a true, invisible, order which could free man from the miserable, encircling, chattering, greedy and bargaining social mass.

'The basic reason for the present situation is the fact that only now have the sciences drawn the final conclusion from the beliefs of the seventeenth-century. This doctrine (derived from the law of the conservation of energy) that mental processes are epiphenomena—will-of-the-wisps on the morass of mindless matter, is the most influential factor in the whole of contemporary literature.'

According to Dilthey, belief in the recently discovered laws of thermodynamics strengthened materialism (and thereby affected our morality) because if they determine what energy is available in the universe, there is no independent force which the mind can exercise and the mind comes to be seen as a by-product (or epiphenomenon) of matter. True or false, this seems to me an interesting theory about the connection between scientific developments and changes in our moral attitudes.

As well as the issues which concerned the whole civilized world there were others, peculiar to Germany, which affected Dilthey. When he was young his country was divided into many principalities most of them governed by hereditary, reactionary autocrats. He saw the unification of Germany, which he strongly desired, accomplished by the military triumphs of Prussia and the imposition of an illiberal regime he disliked, and the harsh priorities of politics, the role of sheer power in history, were impressed on his mind. 'I, too, believe', he wrote to another friend of his, the historian Treitschke, 'that Prussia should remain a military state with a strong monarchical unity and that, together with its blessings, I must bear all the misfortunes of such a situation.'

Dilthey's philosophic efforts were a response to the social, cultural, moral and political climate, but they were also sustained by his insatiable curiosity and love of scholarship for its own sake. To understand what our civilization was like and how its problems arose was only a beginning; the philosopher should also apply the same critical analysis to man's aspirations, to the goals and values which are among his traditions. Philosophy can hold up a mirror to man and tell him what he is and what he wants; the philosopher does not invent new principles or ideals but crystallizes what is implied in the activities of individuals or societies.

The practical use of philosophy in diagnosing our problems and suggesting how we can cope with them presupposed, in Dilthey's view, an understanding of man and his world. He turned, therefore, to what proved to be his most lasting and original achievement—an investigation in depth of how man can know man through everyday contact and through the development of the various human studies. He knew from his own scholarly efforts as an historian that this knowledge could be difficult to attain.

They are truly the tortures of Tantalus [he wrote in a letter quite early

5

in his career] which the historian of Christianity suffers. . . . I struggle in vain to recapture from this strange material what went on in those people's minds. . . their mistrust of human nature in its healthy tranquility which I have always admired; their yearning for the beyond and for super-sensuous knowledge which I hate so much; the life of the sects which I find completely incomprehensible. (*Y.D.*)., p.152).[10]

So how can we understand men of different civilizations or, for that matter, our own fellow-citizens who differ from us in temperament and background? Dilthey's philosophy of the human studies tries to go to the roots of this question. Though general and abstract, his considerations are, nevertheless, of practical importance. The fact that it is not the philosopher's job to devise new questionnaires or test new experimental procedures does not mean that he is fiddling with obstruse problems while Rome is burning, because the success of specific inquiries depends on general considerations. We can only get the right answers to particular questions if our basic ideas are right; we can only be confident that we know what an individual delinquent is like if we have a clear conception of what it takes to know any human being. Philosophic consideration of such issues is not just a boring distraction which keeps us from getting on with the job but an essential preliminary to successful research.

As a matter of fact, Dilthey's work contains many down-to-earth suggestions, because he was not only a philosopher but also an historian, literary critic and student of psychology. He discussed, to give a few examples, the historian's use of letters and diaries, the value of autobiographies for psychology, and offered interpretations of Shakespeare's plays. Interesting though these suggestions are, they do not match his theoretical work in importance. I mention them because it is encouraging to know that Dilthey's theorizing about the human studies springs from familiarity with their practice.[11]   We can now formulate more specifically the question we started with; what is the value of Dilthey's philosophy of the human studies for us today? Before we get down to the details of his exposition it is a good idea to stand back and consider its outstanding qualities. The massive common-sense which pervades Dilthey's whole approach, though often despised because it does not dazzle with amazing new conclusions, is a quality rarer than its name suggests. The student of Dilthey's ideas, once he has understood them, may well say 'but of course' and this is as it should be. We have had our brilliant simplifications now we can do with another dose of balanced common sense. It is cleverly suggestive to make out the case that man is a naked ape, or to demonstrate how much man's behaviour resembles that of pigeons or rats; it requires common sense to insist that man is neither ape nor pigeon and that we must treat him as man.

This is not a trivial issue, for the complaint that modern social science lacks common sense is widespread. Again and again one hears that the topics which are chosen for research, and which attract financial aid, do not deal with important problems, that the methods used for investigating them are out of proportion to the aims, and the conclusions useless. Derogatory jokes to this effect are common; for instance, there is the description of the sociologist as the man who spends half a million on the way to a brothel. Some of this criticism may be prejudice but we cannot dismiss all of it lightly.

Unfortunately any lack of sense there may be in modern social science is not simply dispelled by a child pointing to the emperor's nakedness; otherwise gales of laughter would have swept away these vagaries long ago. The extravagances of the professional students of human nature are well protected by an armour of theory. To destroy it we require theoretical arguments, like those provided by Dilthey, on behalf of common sense.

The common-sense injunction to treat man as man is not just an empty tautology; it warns us against the one-sided views which some scholars have actually advocated. One would have thought that it was hardly necessary to stress that man was not a purely spiritual, altruistic and rational being; but demands implied by such a conception have been made upon man, and a widely accepted social system has been caught out by the fact that people do not work as hard in collective farms for the common good as they do for themselves on small plots. But the other extreme, treating people as animals like other animals, is equally misguided, because it is possible to discuss things with people and even appeal to their better nature.

The kind of balanced, common-sense approach which Dilthey

advocated took man's physical nature into account. He advocated ecological studies and the examination of our biological make-up, but he stressed even more the importance of concentrating on the unique features which distinguish human life from any-thing else in the universe. Only man is able to think abstractly and develop intricate languages which make possible the devel-opment of a complex social life, religion, history, literature and moral codes. These make it necessary to study man in a different way from the rest of nature. Though human beings fall through space like other objects, breathe and feed like other animals, they alone can *tell* us what they think and feel. Familiar though this fact is, it has often been ignored by theories of knowledge and philosophies of science.

Treating man as man and not as a piece of matter or an insect seen through the lens of a microscope, is not only sensible as a method of studying him; it is also a moral imperative. Dilthey reminds us that, in studying ourselves and our fellow-men, we are not dealing with something to be looked at, manipulated and experimented with. Men have an inner life, a point of view of their own, which *they* can express and to which *we* must listen.

So Dilthey tried to work out the implication of the plain fact, obvious to common sense, that in the human world mind com-municates with mind. There the knowing mind is at home among the activities and products of the mind. This creates problems unknown to the sciences. We do not scorn or condemn physical objects or even plants and lower animals and, not being preju-diced, we can study them with detachment. The human world, in contrast, is only too likely to be full of mutual condemnation and prejudice. Conservatives and radicals, religious and irreli-gious, drinkers and abstainers, all see things from their own point of view. Objectivity becomes hard and elusive. But sometimes we have not made enough of our advantages, the full use of which a properly developed methodology should encourage. One of these is that we are familiar with the working of the human mind. No one needs to tell us in terms of hypothetical construc-tions what it is like to be angry or how people are moved by ambition, for we know it from experience, as we shall never know what it is like to be a piece of iron attracted by a magnet.

Dilthey's insistence on the truly human in man, his effort to

8

establish and justify a humanistic approach in the social sciences, is his most important contribution to debates which continue to this day. But there are other aspects of his common-sense approach which deserve separate mention. One of these is his life-long advocacy of an open-minded and flexible response to experience. He was particularly concerned to warn against the various ways in which we distort our observations by preconceived ideas and prejudices, or even exclude sources of knowledge for theoretical reasons. Even today serious scholars have to be warned against jumping to conclusions. One often meets people who think they have discovered examples of racial prejudice, class struggle or latent sex motivation mainly because their theoretical assumptions have predisposed them to do so. Such predispositions also work negatively, so that people refuse to accept evidence because, let us say, it cannot be quantified. The deleterious effect of these various forms of blinkering cannot be overestimated and makes Dilthey's carefully presented case against such bias still worth reading.

Another feature of Dilthey's whole approach, which reflects his own temperament as well as being a matter of deep conviction, is his tendency to see everything within reality as interrelated. This sense of comprehensive unity, which it is man's job to rediscover, has been most succinctly expressed in E.M. Forster's injunction 'only connect'. This too may be put on the credit side of common sense because it is the neat compartmentalization of experience which is artificial and ultimately misleading. In the young Dilthey, however, this sense of unity amounted to a mystic vision which he expressed with the extravagant enthusiasm of youth; for example, after a spring outing, he recorded in his diary, 'I felt as if I had a deeper intimation of the mystical connectedness of our whole world-view with nature' (*Y.D.*, p.121).

Dilthey brought this strong sense of unity, which is superficially reflected by his constant use of the word '*Zusammenhang*' (literally 'hanging together' but best translated as 'context' or 'system'), to all his own research; he was constantly drawn from one problem to a related one and was unceasingly conscious of the bearing different disciplines had on each other. One could not study theology, he felt, without taking account of history and philology, subjecting crucial concepts to philosophic analysis and applying psychology to religious experience. A literary work can only be appreciated properly by considering the social and political circumstances of the time in which it was written and entering into the author's view of the world. For historical understanding he thought a knowledge of geography, psychology and technology was necessary.

Underlying all, was his assumption that reality is a whole of interrelated parts (and not an agglomeration of independent pieces) and that philosophy must make us aware of that unity. 'Philosophy', he wrote, 'is the effort to make us conscious of the unity and connectedness of all the expressions of being' (Vol. VIII, p.180).[12] (The sentence has been abbreviated to exclude references irrelevant in this context.) He applied this idea to every area of scholarship he tackled, anticipating Gestalt psychology and more recent theories of personality by insisting very strongly that the mind is a structured whole and that every one of its operations is coloured by the characteristics of the whole structure. In his analyses of literary works, cultural systems, social groupings, historical phenomena or whole ages, he invariably emphasized that they were complex entities embedded in even more complex contexts. Isolated phenomena, unconnected facts or independent mental acts were, for him, hypothetical constructions, because what we encounter in experience is invariably part of an enormously intricate web.

This is in striking contrast with, and provides a useful corrective to, the strong trend towards specialization which, for reasons familiar to all of us, is unavoidable today, though something may be lost if we do not try to counteract the tendency. Because the mind is embodied in matter, because individuals are enmeshed in society, and single incidents part of the flow of history, more is needed than occasional forays across the borders of the different disciplines. What we need, and what Dilthey tried to provide, is an overall picture of how the various disciplines could work together and supplement each other.

Dilthey's humanistic, down-to-earth and comprehensive approach made him look at the various disciplines concerned with man in a fresh light. He rejected, as most of us would today, the idea that there was a hidden plan, pattern or blue-print for history which a rational study of events could reveal, but considered the view that history was just a meaningless sequence of events ('one damned thing after another')[13] equally unattractive. His solution, characteristic of his whole approach, was that human beings, by their plans and purposes, give what meaning there is to history. To search for meaning in history was, for him, a question of discovering and studying the ideas which prompted human actions. As for psychology, he was anxious that it should avail itself of as wide a range of evidence about human nature as possible, using, for example, autobiographies, chronicles and literature. He also addressed himself to the problem of making psychology useful to various other disciplines—helping the historian to understand the motives of historical figures, or illuminating the creative processes for the literary historian. These are useful goals, not entirely realized even today, so that it is still worthwhile considering how they may be furthered. Dilthey envisaged an anthropology which was a closer integration of the psychological, sociological and cultural studies of man than has yet been achieved.

Dilthey did not confine his sensible, balanced, attitude to his scholarship but extended it to his whole approach to life. He knew that irrational forces were at work in the world but he kept his faith in the efficacy of reason; though he recognized the powers of force and chance in human history, he remained optimistic; he was resigned to the fact that there were limits to the search for knowledge, yet he continued this search with youthful enthusiasm until the end of his life.

These, then, are some of the qualities of mind which determined Dilthey's philosopic approach. To make good the claim that his approach can be of real help to social scientists today, we shall have to reconstruct—from Dilthey's voluminous writings—the main lines of his arguments. First, however, I shall try to explain why the impact of Dilthey's ideas has been delayed and why the intellectual climate has only recently become favourable to them, by saying something about his writings, the way they reached the public, and how they were received.

2

Dilthey's writings and their reception

Dilthey's scholarly knowledge and output are awe-inspiring both in range and quantity. His philosophic writings cover the nature of philosophy, the theory of knowledge (or epistemology), moral philosophy, aesthetics and the philosophy of the human studies, but he also wrote about psychology and educational theory and produced major intellectual biographies and numerous essays on literature.[1] One gets an idea of the quantity of his writings by the fact that his collected works, if ever completed, will amount to some twenty-five large volumes.

This large and varied body of work was made possible by his enthusiasm, curiosity, energy and the single-minded devotion which kept him at his desk for twelve and fourteen hours a day; his capacity to pour out his ideas in a continuous stream was a contributing factor. But the circumstances of a nineteenth-century German professor were also more favourable to scholarship than they are for most modern academics. There were servants in Dilthey's house and he certainly never cleaned his shoes or helped with the washing up. (He probably never set foot in the kitchen.) He also had more control over the timing of his lectures than university teachers have today and could plan his days more efficiently. He was freer than his successors to choose what he taught—which varied according to his interests and current research; as was the custom at the time, his students even helped him with his research by making précis of books for him and taking dictation.

Dilthey's first major publication was Part I of his biography of Schleiermacher which was widely acclaimed as a piece of original scholarship. How he came to write it and what made it such an extraordinary book will be discussed in the next chapter; here it is enough to record that it established Dilthey as a distinguished scholar. His next large work, which appeared in 1883, was Volume I of his *Introduction to the Human Studies*, a work which examined the intellectual foundations of our knowledge of the human world. But, as was the case with his biography, he never published the intended second volume and came to be known as a man of first volumes.

Apart from these substantial works, essays, lectures and papers of his appeared in specialist journals and the proceedings of learned societies. The only other book he published was *Poetry and Experience*, a collection of literary essays which had previously appeared in obscure periodicals. Published in 1905, it introduced his work as a literary historian and critic to a wider public, and made a major impact. The impression it made was recalled by a literary scholar in 1949: 'One must have experienced the publication of this extraordinary book when one was young and impressionable, to appreciate how it affected not only thought about the history of ideas but also the next generation's attitude to art and poetry, and above all how it clarified our relationship to Goethe.'[2] In fact the fame of this book virtually misled a whole generation into thinking of Dilthey as *mainly* an historian of ideas and a literary scholar.

When, in 1911, Dilthey died, quite unexpectedly, he was immersed in creative work, but had only published three books and various essays, none of which revealed the scope of his philosophic thinking. Reputable histories of philosophy at that time only gave a sentence to his work after spending pages on some of his contemporaries. It was possible for Albert Schweitzer to study at Berlin, where Dilthey taught, around 1900 without ever becoming aware of the affinity of his own thought with Dilthey's.

Dilthey also left behind a mass of papers which, to this day, are in the Dilthey archives in Berlin. A brief description of these papers gives an idea of the work which has been, and is still, involved in making Dilthey's writings accessible. They are arranged under the first four letters of the alphabet. *A* is the material for a massive study of the history of the German spirit. It contains work on the development of Prussia, on German music and poetry, on Prussian law and educational theory, and was designed to make his fellow citizens conscious of their heritage and ideals. There are, altogether, ninety folders of up to three hundred pages each. *B*, consisting of forty-eight folders, is the work on Schleiermacher and contains a large quantity of material on his philosophy and theology, collected for the second volume. It includes an early work on Schleiermacher's hermeneutics which Dilthey never published, though he won two prizes for it. *C* contains all the other manuscripts on psychology, theory of knowledge, the nature of philosophy and literary criticism. It includes substantial drafts for Volume II of the *Introduction to the Human Studies* and his later plans for a *Critique of Historical Reason*, one hundred and eight folders, some holding as much as seven hundred pages. *D* is the collection of books which were in Dilthey's possession, many of which have been annotated by him. An often quoted example is the note on the fly-leaf of Mill's *Logic* 'Mill is dogmatic through lack of historical knowledge'.

When a group of Dilthey's closest disciples decided to bring out a collected edition of his work they did not, at first, turn to the mountain of unpublished papers, but concentrated on bringing together his scattered publications. This project, though delayed by the war, was completed in 1924 taking the form of six large volumes. They included the first volume of the *Introduction to the Human Studies*, essays on the history of ideas, among them contributions to his history of the German spirit and—in the last two volumes—Dilthey's treatise on descriptive psychology which had aroused a good deal of controversy, some of his essays on aesthetics, an article on hermeneutics and some discussions of the nature of philosophy. The fifth volume also contained a very long introduction by his disciple and son-in-law, G. Misch, which included quotations from the unpublished manuscripts and attempted the first coherent account of Dilthey's philosophy.

Volume VII, which appeared in 1927, included substantial portions from manuscripts written in the last few years of Dilthey's life and among his most important philosophic writings. The dates of these publications reveal the ironic fact that some of the distinguished thinkers who have acknowledged Dilthey's influence were not acquainted with his most important work. Husserl insisted that he was stimulated by conversations with Dilthey ('not his writing')[3] while Heidegger acknowledged his indebtedness in a work which appeared in the same year as Volume VII.[4] So he did not, and could not, have an adequate conception of Dilthey's philosophy; and his existentialist followers inherited an inadequate interpretation of Dilthey.

Several more volumes appeared in the following years. Volume VIII contained both published and unpublished material on Dilthey's famous typology of world-views, while Volume IX reproduced his lectures on educational theory and Volumes XI and XII brought together further essays on the history of ideas. (Volume X, reserved for Dilthey's moral philosophy, did not come out till 1958.) By 1936, however, the publication of the collected works had come to a halt, though some of his other writings had been made available. In 1932 a selection of the philosophically important exchange of letters between Dilthey and his friend Count York appeared. In the following year Dilthey's daughter, Clara Misch, published some of her father's early letters and diary entries (*The Young Dilthey*), and a collection of his essays on *German Poetry and Music* was brought out.

The posthumous publication of Dilthey's writings stimulated philosophic discussion between different schools of philosophy. L. Landgrebe (a former assistant of Husserl and interested in Heidegger's existentialism) and Misch produced critical and searching works on the relationship between Dilthey's philosophy and that of Husserl and Heidegger.[5] In 1936 Bollnow published a comprehensive account of Dilthey's philosophy, which endorsed, and expanded on, Misch's interpretations.

By then the dominance of National Socialism had gradually brought the study of Dilthey to a halt. Landgrebe, Misch, and many other Dilthey disciples had to leave the country and those who remained were silenced. In fact the Rector of Goettingen said in 1936, 'A man who talks about Dilthey does not belong in a German university'.

After the war, interest in Dilthey only revived very gradually because other philosophic movements held the centre of the stage—such as neo-Marxism, which flourished in various forms, and logical positivism (followed by linguistic analysis) which was largely centred on, though not confined to, the Anglo-Saxon world. The appeal of these movements was equalled, if not exceeded (at least on the Continent), by that of existentialism—powerfully represented by Heidegger in Germany and Sartre in France.

But Dilthey's influence had not been completely eclipsed; in Germany some of his disciples preserved and revived his theories about education and the history of ideas; outside Germany others, who had fled from Hitler, helped to disseminate some of his ideas and encourage translations of his works, but both inside and outside Germany the impact of his philosophy was limited. The fact that his ideas were dispersed over so many volumes deterred all but those readers who were already convinced of Dilthey's outstanding importance; the long period over which these volumes appeared, gradually and in no proper chronological or thematic order, made things worse.

In the English-speaking world there were additional obstacles to the recognition of Dilthey's importance. At best it is not easy to translate philosophic texts from nineteenth-century German into twentieth-century English. In the case of a voluminous writer these difficulties become unsurmountable. Who would translate, who would publish and who would buy twenty volumes of Dilthey? There is also a subtler difference in philosophic style which divides Dilthey from the present-day schools of Anglo-Saxon philosophy and obscures real affinities, such as the down-to-earth empiricism and rejection of cloudy metaphysics, the trust in common sense, and the recoil from dogmatism. The Anglo-Saxon style of philosophizing has tended to be aphoristic and formulated more often than not in papers and articles. The best representatives of this school wrote briskly, colloquially and clearly. Unlike his Anglo-Saxon counterparts, Dilthey, burdened with a sense of the connectedness of all problems, strove to produce large volumes which themselves were to be parts of even larger projects. His actual style is not one of hitting nails smartly on the head, but of verbally exploring a subject by successive reformulations. (Some of this may not be due to deliberate method but to the fact that many of his most interesting views are contained in unrevised manuscripts or dictations.) This style, quite apart from making translation more difficult, has aroused the scorn and suspicion of English philosophers. They have found it hard to appreciate that a man so unlike him in style may be as seminal a thinker as the aphoristic Wittgenstein.

Today the situation has changed and there is ample evidence for an upsurge of interest in Dilthey's work. The original volumes of the collected writings, which had been out of print for years, were reprinted in the 1960s and the publication of further volumes undertaken. Several of these, containing numerous essays (some of which Dilthey had published under pseudonyms), the drafts for the completion of his biography of Schleiermacher and his *Introduction to the Human Studies*, have already appeared and others, including, for instance, his lectures on logic, will follow. Several German monographs, mostly originating as Ph.D. theses,[6] and a long and comprehensive book in English have also appeared in the last few years.[7] Articles on, and references to, him have become more frequent, so how can we account for the re-emergence of interest in Dilthey in spite of the obstacles we have listed?

Three trends in the '60s and '70s appear to have turned attention back to Dilthey[8]—continued interest in existentialist themes, preoccupation with the philosophy of science, and some neo-Marxist developments. Though the heyday of existentialist dominance on the continent has been over for some years, certain aspects of it have continued to influence theologians, sociologists, psychologists, psychiatrists and philosophers all over the world; particularly important among these is the stress on hermeneutics (the art or methodology of interpretation) as a means of getting at the truth, which the founders of existentialism took over from Dilthey. Because Heidegger had developed and used this 'art' it attracted many of his followers. In 1960 the German philosopher, Gadamer, whose style and whole approach owes much to existentialism, treated hermeneutics systematically in his massive book *Truth and Method*, which proved very influential. Gadamer returned explicitly to Dilthey's work, though he may have done it less than justice, because he treated Dilthey as a not entirely consistent forerunner of Heidegger. Since then, hermeneutics has received growing attention, and is on the point of becoming fashionable. This is one reason why people have turned back to Dilthey, the philosopher who had revived the ancient concept of hermeneutics.

The philosophy of science became a favourite pastime of philosophers because many of them were turning their back on metaphysics and wanted to appear hardheaded and down-to-earth. How could they show this better than by studying the successful and practically useful operations of science? The intellectual revolution initiated by the relativity theory and quantum mechanics also posed challenging problems and so opened up a rich field of enquiry. But a philosophy of science, it soon became obvious, must give special attention to the social sciences. They had urgent tasks to fulfil in the modern world but their theoretical basis was far from clear, so their status, methods and concepts became matters for philosophic inquiry. Once philosophers and social scientists had turned their attention to these issues they discovered that Dilthey was a major philosopher who had a great deal to say on the subject.

The role of neo-Marxism in the revival of interest in Dilthey takes a little more explanation. We are all familiar with the fact that Marxism—quite apart from its appeal as a political rallying point—exercises a considerable attraction on modern intellectuals. It appeals to many, particularly the young, because—unlike much contemporary Anglo-Saxon philosophy—it claims that philosophy can be 'practical' by guiding social and political actions in a rational and scientific way. It is a philosophy about man in society, it propounds a methodology for studying social reality and, in defiance of the modern tendency towards specialization, stresses the interdependence of different disciplines and the important role of history among them.

The Marxist approach, as Marxists themselves could not fail to notice, is in these respects identical with that of Dilthey. Of course his work differed from Marxism chiefly because he was less confident of his conclusions (or less dogmatic, according to one's point of view); also he was neither dedicated to the class struggle nor convinced of its central role in history. But, in the context we are now considering, these differences are less important than the parallels. For some Marxists this made Dilthey a rival, an opponent even, much more dangerous than the bourgeois philosophers who had abdicated from the class struggle by concentrating on abstruse theoretical problems. In consequence they attacked him and continue to attack him as a conscious (or unconscious) spokesman of capitalism and German imperialism. These polemics alone have been sufficient to bring him to public attention.[9]

But, for the same reasons that made him appear a dangerous adversary to some Marxists, others, less orthodox, considered him a potential ally. They thought that Dilthey, sharing their practical bias, their concern with man and their historical approach, could supplement Marxist theory where it was at its weakest, namely in the analyses of superstructures, i.e. cultural developments, ideas and ideologies. This view is particularly characteristic of the group of German social scientists which has come to be known as the Frankfurt school and achieved considerable prominence.[10] Among them is Habermas who was involved in various debates about the nature and methods of the human studies[11] and whose books have become prescribed reading for social science students in this country.[12] His effort to combine the insights of dialectical materialism with themes taken from Dilthey (as well as from Freud and American pragmatism) was probably the most powerful single factor in focussing attention on Dilthey's work.

In the end, the fact that over a hundred years after Dilthey's first major publication the printing of his collected works is still incomplete, did not prevent the growth of his influence. But the curious way in which his writings saw the light affected, and continues to affect, the interpretation of his work. The reputation he achieved in his lifetime was mainly based on his historical and literary work, while his philosophy remained unknown, let alone understood; taken out of context those writings which reached the public gave a distorted picture of his thinking.

Although the friends and disciples who were close to him during his old age knew something of his philosophic preoccupations and, in the decades after his death, helped to make them more widely known, they often knew only the one side of his thinking which he had discussed with them and were not acquainted with the manuscripts of his earlier period and so could not appreciate Dilthey's interest in biology, his concern

19

with what he called the systematic human disciplines (i.e. psychology, sociology and politics), and his efforts to rebut positivism. (The old Dilthey was more interested in history, literature and the hermeneutic method.) Perceptive philosophers, like Heidegger or Husserl, could perceive *something* of Dilthey's importance from his publications or from conversations with him, but through no fault of their own they could not form a true picture from the inadequate evidence available to them. By the time the posthumous publications came out, most of his own disciples as well as independent thinkers such as Heidegger and Husserl were unable, or unwilling, to absorb the new evidence and adjust the picture of Dilthey which they had formed years earlier.

Subsequent commentators found it equally difficult to assess Dilthey's work as a whole. Many who admired him as an historical scholar or literary critic were totally unaware of his philosophic writings and the theoretical framework which he had constructed for his research. Others were aware of him as a philosopher of the social sciences but did not appreciate that his theorizing was based on extensive experience of practical research. This is particularly true in the English-speaking world for, until very recently, not a line of his historical, biographical or literary work was available in translation. Scholars who concentrated on a few works also gained an imperfect view of his philosophic allegiances and tended, according to their selection, to conclude that Dilthey was a Romantic, a Hegelian, a Positivist or a neo-Kantian. This is because Dilthey tended to deal with any philosopher as sympathetically as he could and only qualified his agreement in a wider context. He was familiar with these misunderstandings and, in a letter to Treitschke, complained about the misconception that he was an uncritical follower of Schleiermacher, ' . . . my friends are not tempted to draw hasty conclusions from my objective absorption in some cultural trend; but I am amused and annoyed that all the world thinks I bear all Schleiermacher's sorrows in my sensitive soul' (1870, *Y.D.*, p.289).

It would be a mistake to blame historical accident alone for the fact that so many of Dilthey's manuscripts remained unfinished and even more of them unpublished during his lifetime. His own personality was partly to blame. There was an element of secretiveness in Dilthey's nature which made him reluctant to publish his writings and prompted his students to call him 'the mysterious old man'. But he was also weighed down by the vastness of his schemes and felt unable to complete them properly. Never satisfied, he kept on revising his drafts and storing them up for future, even more comprehensive, programmes. A complex and subtle thinker, he struggled with ambiguities he could not fully resolve and continuously revised his ideas to achieve a deeper and more comprehensive vision. Believing that the truth had many facets he recoiled from black and white certainties; his gift of entering sympathetically into different ways of thinking, which made him such a sensitive historian of ideas, made him so open-minded that he continued to explore finely balanced possibilities. The more his work becomes available the more obvious this becomes. In fact, the story of Dilthey's laborious, lifelong struggles to systematize his ideas, and his editors' no less laborious struggles to put his writings neatly together, reflects his style of thinking.

These qualities of mind are irritating to those who seek incisiveness and clarity and have, no doubt, delayed recognition of his importance. But those who think that there is no greater obstacle to the attainment of truth than the uncritical belief that one has already found it, and who suspect that dazzlingly neat and elegant theories simplify or even distort the facts, will consider Dilthey's open-mindedness a virtue. They will appreciate that the very incompleteness of his writings teaches us a lesson about the limitations of our knowledge.

It remains true, though, that the qualities of Dilthey's mind, and their effect on his writings and their publication, makes interpreting him particularly difficult. It is all the more important to base one's interpretations on the whole body of his work, though the temptation to concentrate on some 'significant' texts is very strong. Few critics can be competent to judge his interpretation of Hegel, his assessment of seventeenth-century Spanish literature, his theory of knowledge, and history of hermeneutics (to give just a few examples). As well as the variety, the sheer quantity of his writing is daunting, and one is also put off by the recurrence of similar arguments. But it is not safe to pick out a few works as keys to his entire philosophy, because he saw the whole of his work as a continuous effort to understand the human world. He was not a departmentalized thinker and his theories on particular topics can only be fully appreciated in the context of the widest possible knowledge of his writings; he also made innumerable cross-references so that important points about his theory of knowledge may be found in his aesthetic writing or biographical works, and comments on poetry in his epistemology. Even repetitions are often more apparent than real—a small but significant change alters the emphasis. The fact that a balanced and comprehensive view of Dilthey's total output is desirable, does not make it any easier to achieve; after all, a satisfactory synthesis of his thinking eluded Dilthey himself.

Recognition that no effort or scholarly care is likely to produce a comprehensive and definitive interpretation of Dilthey should neither surprise nor daunt us, for it is true of most great philosophers. Successive generations have seen Plato or Kant in a different and new light. This is likely to remain so with Dilthey.

3

Dilthey the man

In spite of the attention which his thought has attracted, little has been published about Dilthey's life. His daughter's édition of his youthful letters and entries from his diary gives us a picture of his youth and early manhood. (*The Young Dilthey* by Clara Misch 1933). Other selections of letters to his friends are also available, but one looks in vain for published information about his marriage, family life, state of health, financial position or manner of death. Still less has the very curious story of his abortive engagement reached print. His privacy has been protected by his family, friends and disciples. The fact that I could not discover until recently how many children Dilthey had, illustrates how difficult it is to get even the barest biographical data.

However, a vast amount of information is contained in a collection of thousands of letters written by Dilthey, his family and friends. They have been transcribed and arranged chronologically,[1] and now await systematic evaluation. Some of them throw light on his work and its aims, others document his professional career (negotiations about professorships and salary, applications for leave of absence, etc.), others again illuminate his personal life and feelings.

Something can also be learned about Dilthey by talking to the right people. Most of those who knew him personally are, of course, dead. But the disciples of his disciples, men who knew his children and close collaborators, hold chairs in German universities and can throw sidelights on Dilthey's personality.[2]

Nothing that can be discovered about his life is particularly sensational; it was that of a respectable and dedicated scholar who affected history by his thought, not his outward actions. I had to ask myself, therefore, if it was relevant, and indeed proper, to disclose unpublished details of his life in a book which is essentially about his ideas, but my misgivings about prying into what is private have been overridden by the belief, which I have accepted from Dilthey, that an author can be understood better in the context of his life and times and in terms of his personality. It is certainly not my intention to explain Dilthey's theories in terms of his relations to his father or his wife, but I should like to convey something of the human being (his griefs and joys, his foibles and preoccupations) who produced this large body of work. When I read some of the available letters I certainly felt moved by the hopes, anxieties and worries of people long dead. This account may also help the reader to get a picture of what it was like to be a German professor in the Victorian age.

Wilhelm Dilthey was born on 19 November 1833. His father, following a family tradition, was a clergyman at Biebrich on the Rhine and Court preacher to the Duke of Nassau. He was a liberal, protestant theologian strongly interested in history and politics; his son even found philosophic texts in his library. His mother was the daughter of a conductor and was very musical herself. Dilthey inherited a lifelong interest in music from her and during his student years he studied composition and enjoyed playing the piano. His essays, first published in book form in 1932, under the title *Of German Poetry and Music* bear witness to his continuing interest in music, for they contain substantial discussions of Bach, Handel, Haydn, Mozart and Beethoven. He had been enthusiastic about Beethoven since his youth when he wrote about his symphonies 'I feel as if only *there* is my soul in its home land'.

After attending local schools Wilhelm completed his secondary education in Wiesbaden and, in 1852, went to Heidelberg to study theology. After about a year he moved to Berlin, mainly because he was attracted by the richer cultural life, particularly the music. Though he continued with theology, because his parents wished him to become a clergyman, and took some qualifying examinations, he became more and more interested in history and philosophy. Even then he showed an incredible capacity for work and mentions working for twelve to fourteen hours a day. He studied Greek, Hebrew and English and, together with groups of friends, read Shakespeare, Plato, Aristotle and St Augustine, to name but a few. We know about this period of his life from the entries in his diary and the affectionate letters he wrote to his parents and other members of his family.

Gradually it became clear to him that his lack of religious faith—as against his abiding interest in religion—disqualified him from a career as a clergyman. He continued his studies with a view to becoming a scholar and university teacher. Because of his thoroughness and unwillingness to concentrate on any narrow area, his period of study was very prolonged and he had to be supported by his parents, though he did try his hand at school-teaching (and hated it). He was also tempted to become a journalist and did in fact continue to write reviews and articles long after being a fully established academic. These occasional writings, published under pseudonyms and only recently traced to Dilthey,[3] give a fair impression of the width of his interests and spare-time reading. They include not only a first sketch of a life of Schleiermacher and several pieces on philosophers such as Schopenhauer, Schelling and J.S. Mill, but also a very sympathetic discussion of Wagner and reviews of various novels including one of Kingsley's. Conspicuous also are his articles on poets such as Tieck, Novalis, Hoelderlin, Heine and Uhland. This interest in poets remained with him all his life. He wrote on German epic and courtly poetry in the last few years of his life (1907–8) and produced several versions of a hundred-page essay on Schiller between 1895 and 1906. (They are included in *Of German Poetry and Music*.)

During these student years he became interested in the work of Schleiermacher (who died a year after Dilthey was born), and this was to prove crucial for the whole of his subsequent intellectual life. Schleiermacher was one of the group of thinkers—Fichte, Schelling and Hegel were the other most important members—who attempted a development of Kant's philosophy which is usually described as German Idealism. As this movement exercised great influence on German intellectual life it was not particularly surprising that Dilthey found disciples of Schleiermacher among his professors in Berlin. Dilthey's own background and range of interests predisposed him favourably towards a thinker who combined theological and literary interests with his philosophic work, had been active in the regeneration of Prussia after the Napoleonic wars and was also a distinguished translator and interpreter of Plato's dialogues.

When one of Dilthey's professors, who was editing Schleiermacher's letters, died Dilthey was asked to take over the editorship. Soon after that he drew on his growing knowledge of Schleiermacher to produce an essay on his hermeneutics which won him two prizes. This was the real beginning of Dilthey's career as a philosopher for—as he wrote some fifty years later—his work on the essay led him to form his basic ideas. By the time he was editing the third volume of letters he had conceived the plan of writing a biography of Schleiermacher.

In 1864 he submitted his thesis (a shortish work on Schleiermacher's ethics) for which he received his doctorate and then habilitated himself (which means he qualified as a university teacher) with a more general work on ethics. After only a short period of teaching in Berlin he was called to a chair in Basel. At last he was free of financial worries, had colleagues—like Jakob Burckhardt—who appreciated him, and the opportunity for further study. (For instance he attended lectures and laboratory work on physiology.) We have an entertaining picture of him in a letter which the American philosopher and psychologist, William James, wrote his sister in 1867, describing a dinner party at the house of Hermann Grimm:

A soft, fat man with black hair (somewhat like the Renan of the photographs) of uncertain age between twenty-five and forty, with very small green eyes [Dilthey was then thirty-four and his eyes were, in fact, blue] he wore the obligatory frockcoat with *an exceedingly grimy shirt and collar and a rusty old rag of a cravat.* The professor overflowed with information about everything knowable and unknowable. *He is the first man I have ever met of a class of men to whom learning has become as natural as breathing.* He talked and laughed incessantly at the table and gave Mrs Grimm the whole history of Buddhism, and I don't know what other bits of the history of religion. After dinner Grimm and the professor got involved in a heated controversy about the primitive form of natural religion. I noticed that the professor's answers became somewhat tired and then his massive head suddenly fell forward. Grimm called out that he'd better have a proper sleep in his chair. He eagerly consented. Grimm gave him a clean handkerchief which he threw over his face and appeared to go to sleep instantly. After ten minutes Grimm woke him with a cup of coffee. He rose, like a giant refreshed, and continued to argue with Grimm about the identity of Homer.[4]

During this year Dilthey's father died and a letter from his mother to his brother shows a different side of Dilthey, as well as testifying to the bonds of affection within the family:

In our beloved Wilhelm God has given us a helper in our great need and our dear departed a most soothing and loving companion and consoler in his last days. I can only express my soul properly by saying that I implore God that he send me such a rescuer when I am in the throes of death and you such a helper. I cannot tell you what he was and is for me (July 1867*Y.D.* p.250)

In 1868 Dilthey left Basel for a professorship at the small University of Kiel. In some ways he had not found the cultural and political atmosphere of Basel congenial and was glad to return to Germany where he felt he belonged. During this year his letters refer to overwork and ill health. He had made similar complaints during his student years and we shall encounter them again. At that time he also reports that he has grown a beard.

In Kiel a somewhat mysterious and painful episode took place about which Dilthey himself wrote in a letter (to his friend Treitschke, 4 January 1871) which ends:

The painful consciousness will never leave me that I have become the innocent and, in a sense, blind cause of the great misfortune which happened to Marianne. No friend will ever be allowed to understand the motives of the most important and striking act of my life so that, in this respect, my character will have to remain un-understood for all time.

Dilthey met Marianne von Witzleben, who had been a lady in waiting at the Court of Oldenburg, and her friend, Lotte Hegewisch, in 1870. A letter reproduced in *The Young Dilthey* refers to their meeting and social contacts without attributing any special significance to them. But in November of that year, Dilthey wrote to his mother:

For the first time since I left your arms I am wholly and boundlessly happy: last night I got engaged to Marianne von Witzleben. As we walked up and down the room with linked arms I saw the picture of you and me walking up and down long ago in the dusk. Bless us, dear mother; she is as good, steadfast and true as you are and all the wishes of my life have merged into the one to make little Marianne completely happy.

At the end of his letter Marianne added:

My dear Mama,
    Wilhelm has given me permission to call you this and I could not do otherwise: I want to tell you—in a few words—how inexpressibly happy I am: at the moment I can hardly grasp that we really belong to each other! You must bless us ... and allow me to write to you more often and tell you about our happiness when I am a bit calmer again.

She signed herself 'Your happy daughter in law'. The engagement, made public on 21 November was broken off a few days later. Marianne was prostrate and physically ill. Agitated letters were exchanged. Lotte Hegewisch, Marianne's older friend and companion, who also seems to have loved Dilthey, wrote many letters which are still available. Friends and relatives, some of whom seemed to have disagreed with Dilthey's decision, intervened, but to no avail though Dilthey proclaimed that he was deeply unhappy. Marianne lived until 1924 and never married.
    We know one fact which must have been crucial to the break up of the engagement, though it is never explicitly referred to in the correspondence. Marianne was the mother of an illegitimate child and one must presume that Dilthey learned of this after his engagement. No doubt the contemporaries of Queen Victoria took a more serious view of this matter than we would today but how precisely it affected Dilthey and why he considered it an insurmountable obstacle to his sole wish to make Marianne happy remains a mystery; even his friend, Treitschke, his sister and brother-in-law, seem to have been puzzled and unconvinced. His letters are certainly far from clear and, as we have seen in

his letter to Treitschke, he refused to state his reasons explicitly. However, quotations from a very long letter to his brother-in-law give some indication of what went on in his mind.

He starts by rejecting as erroneous the idea that he had acted in haste but adds that though he was quite convinced he was right it would unsettle his conscience if they could not fully understand his point of view. He then talks about a possible meeting with his sister and brother-in-law: 'I wanted us to consider objectively if the present circumstances made a marriage possible. I thought it was desirable and right to do so once Miss Hegewisch and Marianne had raised doubts about my thinking objectively.'

A little later he stressed that his desire for a meeting did not spring

from the need to see my own struggles finished by others but from the firm resolve to subordinate my personal happiness to that of Marianne if the closest members of the family think this marriage morally possible. If they do the fact that my doubts and struggle for clarity have been observed by others would not have hindered me in my firm resolve to make Marianne happy.[5] Gossip in Kiel does not weigh in the scales against Marianne's fate and what it is my duty to do about it. I accept the obligation of an engagement so completely that I could act in a way which you probably think is no longer possible. If I am thrown back on my own moral judgment I must say confidently that it forbids the marriage. My only worry is that this judgment contains subjective elements which the thorough examination of a detached observer might have questioned and which—*it is remotely possible*—my own strict investigation could have revealed as a subjective trait which it was my duty *to ignore*.

After discussing this point further he concludes this section of his letter

May God preserve you from having so heavy a decision placed on your conscience . . .

Something terrible is threatening. On the advice of old friends Marianne and I had decided not to see each other in the next few years and probably even to stop writing, but now Miss Hegewisch has decided to return with her to Kiel quite soon while I remain here. She has rejected my request that Marianne should stay with Treitschke and I have written to him that if it is possible he should try to save us both from this dreadful, agonising and futile interlude. But I must not tell him what Miss Hegewisch's motives are. Her plans, which are certainly meant to being further pressure to bear on me, leave me practically helpless.

The sacrifice which—as I never doubted for a moment, or ever shall—I must make for Marianne is infinitely hard for me to bear. So, with the greatest restraint, I must put up with Hegewisch's half-truths and untruths, her various hints (which are reaching Kiel) that she cannot approve but must respect my actions. I must also put up with the judgments which the intrigue in Treitschke's house at Heidelberg produce. I do not doubt what I have to do but I am suffering immeasurably.

I have looked into an abyss which has made life repellent to me. I have on my conscience the fate of a dear girl, though I am certain that I could not have made a different moral judgment and that I am completely innocent (even if you allow that I may have been careless). However, I realise that guilt, in the sense used by the ancients, of being an innocent cause, is a tragic truth. I cannot explain even to my closest friends how much a decisive action of my life was determined by duty.

No one can miss the implication that Dilthey knew something, unknown to his correspondents, which he refused to disclose for Marianne's sake. We do not know if this was simply the existence of the baby or if there were some additional circumstances which upset him. So we do not have enough evidence to condemn or justify Dilthey's action, though we may suspect he acted with a puritanical idealism which is strange, and even a little repugnant, to us today. Certainly the whole affair affected him deeply for he kept Marianne's letters for many years and only burned them after showing them to his elder daughter. The fact that Dilthey had the poignant experience of having to make an agonising personal decision was worth mentioning in some detail because philosophers are often suspected of being so cloistered in their ivory towers that they never face a graver choice than when to turn off the bath tap.

Dilthey's time in Kiel was also marked by an event of a very different kind which was every bit as important for his life—the publication of the first volume of his biography of Schleiermacher. The culmination of years of work, it appeared in 1870. Though he never abandoned hope of completing this work, the scale on which he planned it defeated him and even the second part of Volume I had to be supplemented by posthumous notes. Volume II only reached the stage of a massive collection of material on Schleiermacher's philosophic and theological work. Postcards and letters written to E. Spranger in the last weeks of Dilthey's life suggesting that they should work together on the biography, provide poignant testimony that this un-finished project weighed on his mind to the end.

What made this biography so interesting, but also prevented its completion, was Dilthey's conception of what the biography of a historically significant figure, be he statesman or original thinker, should be. Such a man, Dilthey believed, powerfully reflected and even transformed the cultural and social forces which have shaped him. So Dilthey considered that nothing that he knew or could learn was irrelevant to his biography. It also followed that nothing that found its place in such a work could be neatly confined to it—but was apt to call for expansion into an independent study.

This is why *The Life of Schleiermacher* gives us a picture of Dilthey's intellectual range and helps us to understand the qualities of his mind. His choice of biography is itself significant and so are the methodological decisions which he analysed and tried to justify in his theoretical writings. It also contains the themes which were to occupy him for the rest of his working life.

Dilthey's historical and biographical work is not an early aberration abandoned when he discovered philosophy was his true calling; the empirical and philosophic were not for him separate activities between which he divided his time as a man may do between banking and golf. A belief in the interdependence of the historical, empirical and philosophic approaches was the corner stone of his thinking. History, of which biography is obviously a branch, interested him for its own sake but he also used it as a basis for philosophic reflection. His attempt at a history of the German spirit, for instance, was intended to provide factual information as well as to clarify the moral ideals of his fellow citizens and point the way for Germany's future. This was, in fact, his most ambitious project, of which the biography of Schleiermacher and essays on German statesmen, poets and musicians, on German law and scholarship (some of which have already been mentioned) were to form part.

Even where his main purpose was philosophical, for example when he was discussing aesthetics, educational theory or the epistemological foundations of the human studies, he approached his subject historically, i.e. by reviewing past ideas on the subject, because he believed that most topics could be illuminated in this way. Even more important for his philosophic thinking than the support which he drew from the conclusions of his historical research was this experience of actually *doing* research. His philosophy of the human studies has the merit of being prompted by problems he himself had encountered and at the same time of analysing methods he used in his own research. This is worth mentioning because philosophers of science are sometimes accused—and not always wrongly—of being back seat drivers who have never held the wheel.

The fact that Dilthey's historical work so often took the form of biography also springs from his personal convictions. He believed that individuals are the ultimate, meaningful, units of society and that their actions shape history. Whatever generalizations the social scientists may aim for, whatever trends the historian may try to discover, the individual is of intrinsic and permanent interest to the human studies. This is why *The Life of Schleiermacher* was only the first of many biographical works which focussed on the intellectual development of poets, philosophers, historians and politicians. His last major work of this genre was *The History of the Young Hegel* (1905) in which he traced the influence of Hegel's theological training on his philosophy.

In the English-speaking world Dilthey's historical and biographical writings—which, together with his literary essays, form a large proportion of his work—have remained almost entirely unknown. Interest in Schleiermacher and even Goethe is limited to specialists outside Germany, so little has been translated apart from two chapters from the Schleiermacher biography, some short excerpts from a Goethe essay and from a few literary articles translated in *Selected Writings* (1976).

Brief summaries cannot convey the content of this type of work or the quality of the scholarship. One can only give a selective list of his subjects. Besides the many articles on German writers already mentioned he also produced essays on Shakespeare, Milton and Dickens, on Cervantes and Calderon, Corneille and Moliere (in *The Great Poetry of Imagination*). He also wrote about the development of philology, psychology, sociology and Christian theology. In tracing the growth of historiography he examined the works of Greek and Roman, French, Italian and German historians. Among the English historians he discussed were Gibbon, Macaulay and Carlyle.

Because the biography of Schleiermacher is so characteristic a product of his penchant for intellectual biography and shows his interests and methods so fully, it deserves a closer look. For Dilthey a man's life, the life of an influential thinker in particular, was a microcosm which reflected the macrocosm of the social and cultural work around him; he was part of the intellectual and political movements which he helped to direct and heir to traditions which he helped to perpetuate, or to which he gave a new twist. He interacted with individuals, institutions and organizations which influenced him and which he, in turn, affected. This is why such a man forms a nodal point of history and why biographies, which themselves need a historical setting, are the essential building bricks of history.

This idea, taken seriously, determined the pattern of the Schleiermacher biography. Dilthey examined the beliefs and religious practices of the Herrenhuters, because Schleiermacher had been brought up within that Christian sect, and the role of the protestant clergy in the Germany of that time, because that is what Schleiermacher became. The fact that Schleiermacher lived in Berlin for a time prompted Dilthey to review the history and cultural atmosphere of that city, and Schleiermacher's friendships with some Romantic poets provided the reason for a detailed account of the Romantic movement and its leading representatives. Because German literature, from Lessing to Goethe, exercised considerable influence on Schleiermacher as it did on most middle-class Germans Dilthey considered its development in detail. He was particularly interested in the fact that all these poets were also thinkers and scholars who consciously shaped a distinctive world-view and ideals of their own. Philosophy too was obviously important in Schleiermacher's development and Dilthey, therefore, gave whole chapters to detailed discussions of the philosophies of Kant and Spinoza. The founding of the University of Halle and the history of hermeneutics are examples of other topics which Dilthey took up because they had a bearing on Schleiermacher's life and work.

Two of the methodological principles embodied in this whole approach are closely related to each other. Once Dilthey had committed himself to the importance of studying unique individuals he had to consider their actions in terms of the parts they were made up of and the larger contexts of which they were part. Explanations had to take account of the mutual interdependence of parts and wholes, for it was only possible to understand a part in terms of its place in a larger whole, yet the whole could only become comprehensible in terms of its parts. This is the methodological basis of the link between history and biography.

One further aspect of explaining individuals in terms of their actual contexts can be formulated as a separate principle which Dilthey invariably espoused. Explanations must, from the outset, take full account of their complex subject matter and not start from generalized assumptions about human nature, the course of history or the basis of society.

Equally important in Dilthey's biographies is what I shall call the double-focus principle. This means that we must assess a man in the light of what his contemporaries thought of him and in terms of the consequences of his actions, but we must also see him as he saw himself, consider what he thought he was doing, what he was aiming at and how he interpreted his world. If we cannot enter into a subject's point of view and the inner life from which his actions originated, we cannot write a proper biography. This is why Dilthey considered the use of letters, diaries and the subject's own writings or lectures of oustanding importance. It was, after all, his work on Schleiermacher's letters which inspired the idea of a biography. In fact Dilthey repeatedly wrote about the problems raised by the use of such material. In the Schleiermacher biography, he considered, for example, how letters are best used in historical research. He stressed that they reflect the occasion on which they are written and the purpose for which they are composed; they are also coloured by the author's conception of and relation to the recipient. So the utmost caution is necessary before we can draw conclusions from them about the author's general views and attitudes. To evaluate letters we must place them into different contexts, i.e. compare them with letters written at the same time but to other people and with those to the same person at other times, as well as relating them to entries in diaries, the letters to which they are a response, and to independent details about the recipient.

It should now be clear how germinal for his whole intellectual life the biography of Schleiermacher, and the preoccupations it forced him into, turned out to be. The study of German thought, to which Schleiermacher had made important contributions, the German literature which had influenced him and the subject of hermeneutics on which he had lectured in Halle, all continued to occupy Dilthey's mind.

His years in Kiel, which had been marked by his abortive engagement and the publication of *The Life of Schleiermacher* came to an end in 1871 when he received a call to a professorship in Breslau. A new and fruitful chapter of his life opened. One of the important events of that period was his meeting, soon after he had settled in Breslau, with Graf York of Wartenburg. A close friendship, which enriched both his personal life and his work, developed and lasted until York's death in 1890. York was a landowner who, as a member of the aristocracy, took an active part in politics, but was also a scholar of distinction with a penetrating philosophic intellect. Dilthey wrote to him about his ideas and plans and York offered sympathy, encouragement and, at times, vigorous critical comment. Dilthey often stayed on York's estate or met him elsewhere and they spent long hours talking philosophy. Dilthey admired his friend's intelligence, moral incisiveness and clarity of mind enormously and never seems to have taken issue with remarks which appear to be very strongly in conflict with his own philosophy of history. I am thinking, for instance, of a remark by York that it was 'very significant that Zeno was of Semitic blood'. The two men also exchanged family news and chatted about the trivia of daily life. Dilthey frequently, and in some detail, refers to his health. In fact, the editor of the correspondence[6] states that he has omitted 'Dilthey's numerous and characteristic complaints about his

35

health'. Such discussions among friends were apparently a common expression of intimacy at that time. It appears that Dilthey was not particularly delicate but suffered periodically from overwork and nervous complaints not uncommon among highly creative people. On one occasion York tells him 'the discomfort of your state is caused by constant sitting and is not a direct result of strenuous thought'.

On 19 November 1873—amost three years to the day after his first engagement—Dilthey became engaged to Katharine Püttmann, a lawyer's daughter, whom he had come to know three months before. Again he writes in most exuberant terms. For instance, in announcing his engagement, he says 'I have been overcome by the most selfless, all-powerful love which would like to die for the beloved'. To her he writes on the same day: 'It is so dull here that I hardly dare to say how I feel, with what infinite longing I count the hours until I can hold my happiness in my arms again . . . Käte, my Käte, I embrace you a thousand times in thought and can hardly compose my mind to think of anything but you.' The archives contain bundles of letters in a similar mood covering the period up to their marriage on 21 March 1874. A letter to Käte's mother from that period is noteworthy. He had been for a medical examination because of some unspecified worry about his health.

My conscience demands that at our official engagement no concern about my health should exist and this has upset me terribly. Not that I was seriously worried about a major illness developing, but I do not want to bring even the slightest chronic ailment to my marriage with Käte as I am generally so healthy. Everything in my body promises a long and healthy life and I would not have given the matter a second thought. But at present I am only thinking of how I can combine everything within me to make Käte as infinitely happy as she deserves and as my love for her demands. I know, of course, that all our happiness lies, ultimately, in the hands of fate and that there are limits everywhere to what seems limitless: only noble character and deep love, I know, are wholly reliable.

The Diltheys had three children. Clara, her father's favourite and later his helper and confidante, was born in 1877. Max, whose health caused repeated worries was born in 1884, and

Helena (Lenchen) in 1888. But the marriage was not without
its troubles. One reason, apparently, was that Dilthey wanted to
do nothing but work while his wife wanted a little
pleasure—travel, outings and entertaining. Her desire to enjoy
herself even while she was pregnant greatly upset Dilthey's
mother who, by all accounts, was a kindly soul. Dilthey's mother
and sister thought Kätchen should take it easy and be more
careful but the latter was not pleased by such interference.
Dilthey's sister wrote to him (1883): 'I am deeply aggrieved for
our dear mother; she is upset and unsettled daily which affects
her state of health . . . The other letter this morning was from
Käte and its second half caused us all, but *particularly* poor
mother, real annoyance. You must see yourself how little consideration and sensitivity she shows towards mother . . .' Later
she complains that they 'have been treated without consideration
or sufficient candour. Clara also revealed—long after her parents'
death—that they had such severe rows that she—Clara—
implored them to get a divorce as the upsets made her father
incapable of work for days. However, the couple stayed together.
Käte's health was not very good—she had lung trouble—and her
husband showed his concern by, for example, staying with her
on vacation instead of returning to the University at the beginning
of term. There is also ample evidence that his wife helped him
with his work. Sometimes, particularly on holiday, he dictated
to her and some of his letters are in her handwriting. On other
occasions she wrote on his behalf.

Dilthey's major intellectual preoccupation during his years in
Breslau was the nature and methods of the human studies—the
area of scholarship in which he made his most famous contribution. Using plans and drafts he had started as early as 1866
(now published in Volume XVIII) he produced in 1875 *The
Study of the History of the Disciplines dealing with Man, Society
and the State* (Volume V). Above all, he did most of the work
on Volume I of *The Introduction to the Human Studies* (published
1883) and on the drafts for the second volume (due to be published
in Volume XIX).

In 1882 Dilthey crowned his academic career by returning to
Berlin to occupy the chair of philosophy which Hegel had once
held. As he took up residence in Berlin he wrote enthusiastically

to York about his new flat: 'The flat is really enchanting. From my desk I look across our garden to a sheet of water thickly fringed by trees'. He was to remain in Berlin until the end of his life, changing flats a few times and living in an affluent upper middle-class style. He was by now fairly well paid (the salaries of professors were, as they are to this day in Germany, subject to negotiation) and earned a useful income from the numerous articles and reviews he contributed to journals. References in some letters also suggest that there was a little inherited money in the family. There were several servants in the house and Dilthey's wife had a wet nurse (at least for her third child). They did not, however, have a carriage of their own. A hired vehicle took Dilthey to the university and he composed his mind for his lectures during the journey. On the whole Dilthey was very content in Berlin, particularly when he could concentrate on his scholarly work. Thus he wrote to York in the summer of 1884: 'I am leading my summer life. I meet people only professionally; otherwise I live with my books on my balcony or in my garden which is full of roses, or in the Grunewald. I wish I could turn my back on the world entirely, like you and Carlyle. For my old age, if I should reach it, I have no other thought except complete withdrawal from the world.' Sometimes, though, he complains about the philosopher's fate (February 1884): 'I could envy a woodcutter for being able to see every day, every week, what he has accomplished. The demands on the man who philosophises cannot be fulfilled. A physicist is a pleasant reality, useful to himself and others: the philosopher exists, like the saint, only as an ideal.'

Even more bitterly than about the problems of philosophic achievement he complains about the routine duties of his professorship. 'Since March', he wrote to York in July 1890, 'I have been running like a donkey on a treadmill—tired, often giddy and with something pressing on my head'.

The letter then lists the professorial chores which he found largely unwelcome, at least compared with his scholarly work. The list does not differ strikingly from the duties of an English university teacher today but, as the staff-student ratio was probably much more adverse, larger quantities of written work of all kinds had to be marked or assessed. Dilthey mentions that he is lecturing ten hours a week and also preparing a new course. He had twice-weekly committees and fortnightly examination essays and course work to mark. Ph.D. theses and applications for habilitations had to be considered and prize essays judged (which, he complains, took weeks of work).

In 1896 he again reported a serious illness which he himself described as of 'nervous origin'. In that year he was also worried about his wife's health as well as that of his son. He suffered at times from insomnia but continued his tremendous programme of research and writing. He speaks of getting up at 4 a.m. and writing for twelve hours. One of the projects he had taken up, as we learn from the letters of that time, was the continuation of his biography of Schleiermacher.

An account of his personal moral convictions, which he vividly expressed in a letter to his twenty-year-old daughter may also be of interest (though it may also remind the modern reader a little of Polonius' speech).

Be good my dear child; the consciousness of having always acted, as far as one knows, honestly, purely and according to what one owes to one's own character and the welfare of others is the sole, indestructible, absolute good of man. Then he can face anybody freely. Closely related to this is—give to your existence an inner value through your own inner life and think always of the more beautiful, higher, world of mind'.

At times his responsibilities weighed heavily on him. About 1900 he wrote to his daughter:

How tired I am of the difficulties of life which keep recurring in spite of all my efforts. I never wanted anything for myself but only for my family and for the circle of duties and goals within which I live and work. Activity was always my greatest happiness but now I feel so tired.

We have reached the time—the early years of the twentieth century—about which we have the written and oral testimony of some of his most distinguished pupils. Indeed, only a few years ago it was possible to talk to some of them—as well as to his daughter.

As a lecturer his students thought of him as quiet but impressive. He struck them as rather taciturn, enormously learned, dedicated and a little mysterious. Even his closest collaborators only had glimpses of particular schemes and did not know all he was working on. We have already seen, when talking about his personal life, that he was not an easy man to understand. There is no doubt, however, that he was greatly loved and respected.

After 1900 he gave up his seminars and by 1905 he had withdrawn from public teaching altogether. For many years, right to the end of his life, he maintained some sort of contact with selected students; this may appear strange to us today but it was undoubtedly of mutual benefit. Nohl gives a vivid account of this practice:[7]

He had established for some time the practice of getting individual students to come to his study as helpers; here they read to him, made excerpts for him, took dictation, added something in writing and, above all, received a curiously free brief to make corrections. We arrived in the morning towards eight and usually found him cheerfully sitting at his desk; then we worked without a break until lunch. After the meal he lay down for an hour: we read to him until he fell asleep and then we made excerpts. He started to dictate again and went on until evening. He stood by the stove or the window and 'composed' as we used to say. In between we read aloud. For the young people it was deeply exciting, particularly because they often did not know the context to which the dictations belonged and had no full view of his philosophy as a whole because Dilthey's works were not easily accessible. In the evening we plunged into the subject just dealt with, in order to keep our heads above water, and next day found ourselves with him at an entirely different spot ...

In a sense Dilthey exploited his students ruthlessly to promote his own work; he asked them to look up things and prepare work which he sometimes used, incorporating it, partly reworded, into his own text. They were, clearly, under constant pressure to take an interest in whatever was closest to Dilthey's heart at the moment. It is equally clear that the students undertook these chores willingly and found this kind of practical apprenticeship exciting and educationally valuable.

With advancing age Dilthey became, if anything, even more

active intellectually and produced a considerable body of important work. His analysis of Hegel's development, his long essay on
the nature of philosophy, his final version of the theory of world-
views, various shorter pieces and, above all, his work on *The
Construction of the Historical World in the Human Studies* stems
from the last few years of his life. In an article about another
scholar he wrote: 'For people like us who research, collect and
reflect slowly, old age is the maturity of life.' He continued to be
full of youthful enthusiasm and of plans for future work. He
wanted to live to one hundred and ten to be able to complete his
schemes, the biography of Schleiermacher among them. Dilthey
was holidaying in a hotel in Seis on Schlern (which is in the
Tyrol) where an infection was raging and the hotel was emptied
by death or hasty departures. The old professor, absorbed in his
studies, did not even notice. He caught the infection and died
unexpectedly on 30 September 1911. The young student who
helped his widow to make the funeral arrangements achieved
some distinction as a philosopher later on. He was Martin Buber.

4

The philosophy of life

Dilthey described his philosophy as a philosophy of life, consciously aligning himself with a group of thinkers some of whose general ideas he shared though he disagreed with others. His disciples, and some commentators after them, have used this label as an exclusive name for his philosophy. So, to get a first impression of his philosophic intentions we must consider what he meant by choosing life as his subject matter.

The most important point is that by life he meant human life. 'In the human studies I use the expression life', he wrote, 'only for the human world' (Vol. VI, p.314).[1] Philosophically he is not especially concerned with the features which all living creatures have in common, nor does he give special emphasis to man's biological make-up. In this he differs markedly from other philosophers of life like Nietzsche and Bergson. There is nothing eccentric about his use of the word. When a housewife complains that she would like to see more life she is not pining for the sight of earthworms or pigeons.

By life he meant the collective life of mankind (what he sometimes called 'social, historical, reality'), rather than life and the psychological processes of individuals. In fact he criticized other philosophers of life, like Nietzsche, for giving too much stress to the personal and subjective at the expense of history and so mistaking 'their own corner for the world' (Vol. VIII, p.196).[2]

For Dilthey life is intellectually and culturally structured. We must not, he thought, contrast intellect and culture with life (as some modern irrationalists have done) because they are an integral part of it. Highly characteristic of his conception is the

42

double title of Volumes V and VI, *The World of Mind. An Introduction to the Philosophy of Life*. This makes it clear that life must be understood in terms of its involvement in the world of mind (i.e. the cultural sphere), a concept which will be explained in the next chapter.

But Dilthey's emphasis on life reflects two important aspects of his whole approach which have already been mentioned. One is his insistence that philosophy must be relevant to life, to the bustling activity of the market place and not just arid speculation which because it does not look beyond the study or the classroom, is 'remote from life'.

The other aspect of Dilthey's approach, pinpointed by his use of *life* is that experience is the sole basis of our knowledge and the only proper subject for the philosopher. So life, the totality of our experiences in contrast to second-hand information, must be the philosopher's guide.

Before we can discuss in detail how Dilthey developed his practical, empirical philosophy of the human world, something must be said about his general view of the nature and functions of philosophy. Philosophers are likely to reflect on what they are doing, and their conclusions will affect *how* they set about their philosophizing. Dilthey gave a great deal of thought to this. It crops up in many of his writings and is dealt with systematically and at length in *The Nature of Philosophy*, a work of 1907 contained in Volume V, and his *Typology of World-Views*, written in 1911 and published, together with earlier works and drafts, in Volume VIII. It is a hallmark of his whole approach that he looks at philosophy from both inside and out. Like other philosophers Dilthey examined the nature of philosophic arguments, the strength or weakness of various philosophic assumptions and the power of various branches of philosophy to make progress in their own sphere. This is what I call the inside view; but he also looked at philosophy as a historian, psychologist and student of the human world in general (in other words, from outside). So he was interested in the way philosophic systems are conditioned by, and reflect, the personalities of their authors and the conditions of their time. He was equally concerned with questions about the functions which philosophy performs in the life of individuals and societies. This double approach should be kept in mind but it would be difficult and pointless to try to disentangle the two approaches at every stage. After all, throughout his writings Dilthey deliberately combined empirical scholarship with philosophic reflection, one of the characteristics which make his work original.

Philosophy for Dilthey was a response to very real and universal human impulses. It fulfils individual needs and serves social purposes. He therefore considered that intellectuals who think that there is a conflict between being philosophical and 'getting down to brass tacks' are profoundly mistaken. 'The pretended sophistication', he wrote, 'with which our bureaucrats and our bourgeoisie turn from ideas and their philosophic expression is not a sign of realism but of spiritual poverty' (Vol. II, p.91).[3]

Dilthey saw men confronted by what he called 'the enigmatic face of life'; they find themselves enmeshed in circumstances they do not understand and suffer pain, death, or separation from their loved ones. In their own lives, as well as in history, they see irrational forces and blind chance at work. Even their own impulses can be puzzling and frightening so they ask what life is all about. What they seek is a coherent picture of reality, ideals to strive for and principles to guide their conduct. Dilthey called this man's metaphysical impulse. Religion and poetry, are, according to him, responses to this impulse. When the response is based on sustained and critical thought it becomes philosophy.

Among the various functions of philosophy he listed is the traditional role of consoling and fortifying the individual in his troubles, to make him—in the popular sense of the word—'philosophic' in adversity. 'If', he wrote, 'we are to bear illness, death or banishment, a special frame of mind is needed in life. Most people receive this from religion; once dogmas have been discredited the educated classes need a substitute which is based on religious or philosophic reflection' (Nachlass, C76, p.21).

But philosophy must not only reassure and strengthen man in his encounters with life's suffering and perplexities; it must also provide both individuals and communities with guidance in their choices and help to improve the quality of their actions.

Every genuine philosophy must, from its theoretical insights, deduce principles for the conduct of the individual and the guidance of society. So action is the goal, even of philosophic comprehension. A philosophy which does not give rise to rules for action or speculation about the work and does not include a view of life and impulses towards regulating it is totally unsatisfactory. It is the task of a practical philosophy to determine what has meaning and value in life; its subject matter is the supreme principles which determine the direction and set the goals of practical action. (Vol. X, p.13)[4]

The crucial process by which philosophy could, in Dilthey's view, promote its essential aims was reflection which leads to more critical awareness of oneself, one's activities and the values and aspirations of a whole community. This point is made repeatedly in his writings and a few quotations will illustrate the aspects of reflective awareness which he stressed. 'Philosophy', he wrote, 'is the developing consciousness of what man does in his thinking, creating and acting' (Vol. VIII, p.38).[5] 'Progress in philosophy', he therefore concluded on the very next page, 'lies in the growing consciousness the human mind, seen as a whole, has of its doings, goals and presuppositions' (Vol. VIII, p.39).[5] He made the same point about communities and cultures: 'The highest achievement of philosophy is to make the culture of an age conscious of itself, and, by clarifying it systematically, heighten its power' (Vol. III, p.25).[6] Or, again, 'It is the function of philosophy to make conscious the impulses of a culture and so make its goals clear, strengthen its will power and formulate the ultimate generalizations of its acquired concepts' (Vol. II, p.322).[7]

In stressing the importance of self-awareness Dilthey followed an old tradition. Through the ages philosophers, religious leaders and poets have considered the imperative 'Know thyself', inscribed on the temple of the Delphic oracle, important because man can only achieve the dignity of being completely human by following this injunction. But this is a different kind of knowledge from knowing if a fungus is edible because, though this may be a matter of life and death, it does not raise philosophic problems. Knowing myself is not only a matter of observation and intros-pection but also of deciding what I consider significant. The choice to be made is creative. What we decide to emphasize will influence what we are and how we act. For instance, when philosophers defined man as a rational animal they meant much more than that he was capable of using reason, for they knew that he could also be unreasonable. They claimed that philosophic reflection shows that reason is an essential part of man which it is proper for him to obey. Dilthey was very much preoccupied with this issue because he was more fully aware than many of his predecessors how intricate are the problems relating factual knowledge and its philosophic evaluation. He saw history and the social sciences as means of self-discovery, but said they must be approached with 'philosophical intent',[8] so that the knowledge thus gained can, in turn, guide man's valuations and choices.

If philosophy is to aid man's self-examination it must also take a further step and examine his various activities. Almost every significant human activity has become the subject of critical inquiry, sometimes forming a separate branch of philosophy—the philosophy of history, aesthetics and political philosophy are obvious examples from an almost endless list. In each case a philosophy is the critical examination of the principles which govern an activity and the concepts we use while engaging in and talking about it. This philosophic reflection has a dual function; by clarifying principles, concepts and methods it is supposed to improve human activities. But the study of his various activities also increases man's knowledge of himself. So the philosophy of law, to take just one example, should not only help us to legislate, train lawyers or conduct trials more efficiently, but also highlight man's nature as a creature living under laws of his own making. In this context Dilthey made one further point of interest. Ascertaining the facts and reflecting philosophically on them, cannot be neatly divided between specialists. For instance, a philosopher concerned with the aesthetic principles of poetry can, and perhaps *must*, use the information given by literary historians. Unless he does, his conclusions are bound to be one-sided. On the other hand, one cannot imagine his doing anything worth while if he has never read a poem. The philosopher who, like everybody else, looks at life directly cannot and need not rely entirely on specialists; from this there follows a further conclusion, close to Dilthey's heart. The philosopher looking at a particular phenomenon—at poetry, religion or at law—from his own point of view has something special to contribute to the subject over and above the critical clarification of concepts or methods.[9] However, describing philosophy as reflection about man and his activities does not fully explain how it fulfils its various functions. Man's metaphysical impulse craves a *Weltanschauung* (a world-view) which combines a coherent picture of reality with an ideal of life and principles of conduct. Myths and religions provide such world-views and so do literary and political works. Philosophic systems present world-views in an abstract and closely argued way.

Because of their central role in philosophy and their tremendous historical importance (well illustrated by the effects of Christianity or Marxism in human affairs) world-views especially interested Dilthey. He was fascinated by the familiar, yet vexing, fact that world-views vary so widely and conflict so sharply even when they are based on the reasoned arguments of philosophers. The history of philosophy showed him a succession of philosophic systems constantly at war with each other, a war in which none of the major contestants has been eliminated and none has proved wholly triumphant. This has often made people sceptical of the claims of philosophy, and presents a special challenge to the historian of ideas, which Dilthey took up in his typology of world-views. He wanted to assess their merits and limitations and to account for their differences.

He started from the belief that world-views which have been widely accepted and stood the test of time must contain elements of truth. Each reveals a genuine aspect of reality but is also onesided because the human mind is limited and conditioned by circumstances. 'We can only', as he put it, 'glimpse the pure life of truth in various broken rays.' He thought the reason the various philosophies conflicted with rather than supplemented each other lay in their tendency to make exclusive claims. This, too, is inevitable. World-views, in order to fulfil their functions, must provide comprehensive answers.

Dilthey then turned to a systematic examination of the reasons why philosophic systems differ from each other. One of the more obvious and non-controversial reasons is that they are all at different stages in their development. The very effort which philosophers make when reasoning, implies that they consider improvement possible. So philosophies differ in their profundity, coherence, comprehensiveness and sophistication. For example, Dilthey thought critical philosophy differed from dogmatism because it was at a more advanced stage in the development of philosophy.

Such advances are often historically determined in the sense that they have become possible through the work of predecessors. But history, in Dilthey's view, played an even more decisive part in accounting for the variety of world-views. 'Every world-view', he wrote, 'is historically determined and, therefore, limited and relative' (*The Dream*, Vol. IV). He said this because he was convinced that the traditions and the knowledge of an age, the state of its science and its economic and social circumstances, all condition man's outlook. He was firmly committed to this historical point of view and the relativity of all beliefs which it implied. Indeed he welcomed this 'historical consciousness' as a remedy for narrow, dogmatic, views. But for him—as for all relativists—it raised general problems about the possibility of reliable knowledge.

There is usually a number of possible and plausible answers to any philosophic problem—indeed they are often simple logical alternatives—and this adds to the variety of world-views. We can stipulate one god or many, treat reason or experience as the main source of knowledge, describe the order of the universe as causal or purposive, decide that morality is about happiness or about duty. So philosophies and world-views in general differ because they adopt one or other of these possibilities.

But the most interesting part of Dilthey's analysis of the differences between world-views is the role he ascribes to personal factors in the choices of alternatives. World-views—he argued—reflect the personalities of those who create or adopt them. This is not to be considered a fault which greater care could eliminate, but the inevitable result of philosophies involving reflective self-awareness. Dilthey considered that this made it possible to classify the world-views in terms of the types of personality reflected in them. In his classification of personalities he distinguished people according to whether thought, will or feeling was their predominant feature. All human beings possess all three and therefore all world-views reflect and take account of man's thoughts, feelings and aspirations. But one of them must—Dilthey thought—become the dominant principle if a philosophy is to be properly unified; which of these it is, is determined by its author's personality.

So Dilthey arrived at a three-fold classification of world-views—and thereby of philosophic systems—for which he became particularly well known. Where thought is dominant we get positivism or materialism which reflects the temperament of a sober, down-to-earth investigator of nature. Under this heading Dilthey listed the philosophies of Democritos and Hume, of Mill, La Mettrie and Marx. What Dilthey called the idealism of freedom reflects the active will of strongly moral personalities; Judaism and Christianity are examples of this world-view and, within philosophy, Kant is its outstanding representative. Dilthey's third type is objective idealism; its central principle is feeling and it embodies an essentially aesthetic, comtemplative, vision of reality. Buddhism is such a world-view and so are the philosophies of Spinoza, Schelling and Hegel.

Dilthey fully appreciated that his classification of world-views—like all classifications—could only be a rough approximation and could not replace close examination of the unique qualities of individual philosophies. He was also aware, indeed he stressed, that such a typology was in some ways arbitrary, simply a way of focussing attention on different issues. As a matter of fact he even mentions different ways of grouping philosophies; but he used his classification to show not only how personal factors affect philosophic thought but also to bring out the typical strengths and weaknesses of different philosophic positions.

More important, however, than the particular typology which Dilthey adopted, was his underlying assumption that it is impossible either to choose between philosophic systems or to combine them in more comprehensive systems. Because they reflect the different points of view of different ages and personalities they cannot be rationally proved or disproved so their claim to be wholly true is open to scepticism. Dilthey welcomed this consequence of historical and psychological relativity because he thought that it liberated man from the shackles of rigid and dogmatic philosophic systems and asserted the mind's sovereignty over its temporary creations.

But he could not resign himself to a complete relativism and the resulting radical scepticism. He retained the idea that philosophic systems reflected aspects of the truth because he realised that complete scepticism is self-defeating. If all philosophic assertions were distorted by their historical and psychological origins and, therefore, unreliable, the statement that this was so would itself be unreliable and the idea of truth become meaningless. Dilthey avoided this by accepting that philosophy, if it is not to liquidate itself and all knowledge, must cling to the idea that our basic thought processes and the rules, such as those of logic on which they are based, are essentially self-validating. In other words, we cannot think without assuming that thought can reach valid conclusions. Like Kant before him Dilthey presupposed that knowledge of the external world, and of what is good and worthwhile, is possible and considered it the philosopher's job to find out what makes this so, thus producing a theory of knowledge which can be applied to the philosophy of science.

It is the task of philosophy [he wrote] to make our everyday assurance about our world the subject-matter of a systematic and exhaustive epistemological critique. This must be extended to the sciences, to psychology, history, to our knowledge of society and to the question of how much our knowledge of reality depends on thought and, finally, to our consciousness of life itself as the source (after the eclipse of everything transcendent) of our ideals and valuations. (Nachlass, C76, p.64)

So Dilthey, though he had rejected the possibility of philosophic systems which presented incontestable world-views, stuck to the conviction that some of its branches such as logic and epistemology could achieve solid results. In his view they could be as scientific as the scientific disciplines of which they are the theoretical basis.

Now that we have an idea of how Dilthey conceived the nature and functions of philosophy and what he thought about its capacity to achieve reliable results, we can fill these outlines in a little. He did not present his philosophy of life as a systematically argued world-view because he did not believe that this could be validly done but he did reflect on most of the traditional philosophic problems from a consistent point of view and so produced a coherent philosophy of his own.

In developing his own philosophy Dilthey drew extensively on the history of philosophy. Here he did not differ from other philosophers except, perhaps, in two respects; he was tolerant and open-minded and his enormous learning allowed him to draw on a wide and varied range of arguments. He tended to pick out what he considered valuable from other philosophers rather than to attack their weaknesses, and he incorporated in his writings various ideas and arguments gleaned from many sources though this does not mean that he was uncritical. His approval of various philosophies, even those with which he sympathised most, was carefully qualified so it would be unfair to call him an eclectic, for he transformed and made his own the ideas he took from others.

Like most modern philosophers he considered the slant towards the theory of knowledge which Descartes had given to philosophy irreversible. He saw himself as an heir to the epistemological tradition and admired many of its exponents, among them Locke and Hume. He praised and felt himself indebted to the great seventeenth-century rationalists, to Leibniz as one of the great representatives of German thought and to Spinoza as the thinker who had profoundly influenced Goethe and Schleiermacher. But the philosopher who influenced him most was probably Kant with his synthesis of empiricist and rationalist ideas. Naturally, he was also affected by the idealist and romantic philosophies of his predecessors Fichte, Schelling, Hegel, the brothers Schlegel, Coleridge and Carlyle.

One of the basic features of any philosophy is its view of the nature of ultimate reality, its metaphysics. But Dilthey rejected the idea that philosophy could give an adequate and reliable account of reality because this involves making unjustified assumptions such as that our perceptions mirror reality accurately or that our reason is equal to the job of grasping reality because the latter itself is rational. For this reason, Dilthey eschewed metaphysics but sketched out a largely negative conception of reality like the negative theology of mysticism. (You cannot explain God's nature, but you can specify what he is not.) The richness and variety of reality cannot—he believed—be properly captured by our conceptual schemes and scientific theories. Though we cast intellectual nets which we try to make finer and finer, reality remains elusive: certainly we are catching *something* in these nets. Indeed the pragmatic successes of science suggest that we are doing better and better. But, unlike many of his contemporaries who believed that the completion of knowledge in various spheres was just round the corner, he thought we could only approximate to, but never reach, the truth. In this respect he anticipated a conception of knowledge which is widely held today by scientists and social scientists.

So Dilthey's conception of reality merges naturally into his theory of knowledge. The nature of reality must determine how we can know it, but the reverse is equally true; until we have ascertained our capacity for knowledge we cannot make claims about the nature of reality. The cornerstone of Dilthey's theory of knowledge is Kant's doctrine that we can only know reality as the content of our consciousness. In this sense the whole world is an appearance or phenomenon. This has nothing to do with the deceptiveness of illusions—when a tree looks like a man in the dark, for example. We are talking about the real world of oceans and forests, of people and things, which is objective because it appears much the same to all of us; so, we can communicate with each other and check our impressions while optical illusions can be corrected by other observations. But this is not the world of ultimate reality but reality as it presents itself to us through our senses and is interpreted by our thoughts. Our knowledge is genuine but, because it is seen from an inescapable human perspective, cannot lead us to ultimate reality.

From this Kant drew a further conclusion adopted by Dilthey, though in a modified form. If the world is reality as it appears to us, then it is reasonable to attribute some of its features to the nature and activity of the perceiving mind. Knowledge cannot be a free creation if it has to be distinguished from fantasy but it is partly the product of the mind's activity in shaping, organising and structuring its material. So it becomes the job of the theory of knowledge to examine the knowing subject, and the self-awareness which Dilthey saw as one of the main aims of philosophy here assumes a specific function. But while Kant and, as Dilthey believed, most epistemologists, concerned themselves with a pure cognitive consciousness, with an observer or thinker in whose 'veins no real blood' but only 'the diluted juice of reason' flowed (*Introduction to the Human Studies*, Vol. I, p.xviii), he was interested in real flesh and blood human beings who were in touch with reality through their sensations, feelings, thoughts and acts of will.

From these contacts with reality, i.e. from experience, all our knowledge is derived, not only knowledge of the outer world but even of the self which did the experiencing. This was the conviction which made Dilthey a thoroughgoing empiricist, but his empiricism took a distinctive form which is best understood in terms of his rejection of speculative knowledge (which we have already encountered) on the one hand, and his criticism of other forms of empiricism on the other. Dilthey was convinced that we could not discover by speculation anything lying behind the sum of our experiences which we call life. 'Thought cannot go behind life' (Vol. V, p.5).[8] 'Life must be interpreted in its own terms' (Vol.V, p.370);[9] quotations like these could be multiplied from his writings.

But Dilthey also rejected the empiricism of the British School and the positivism which developed from it. Because it defined experience in terms of sense perceptions this type of philosophy, in Dilthey's view, imposed its own type of metaphysical strait-jacket on the rich and varied flow of experience. Instead of opening their minds to what they were actually experiencing, these thinkers, according to Dilthey, approached it in terms of the dogmatic presupposition that experience is only what the senses convey. There is, as Dilthey very clearly saw, a special difficulty about this presupposition. What we actually see are not sense data like colour blots but complex objects and events like buses going by. Could our senses by themselves produce the picture of a bus in our minds? This is unlikely for various reasons; for instance we could not claim that we have seen a bus if we did not take it for granted that it had an engine under its bonnet and seats inside or that it normally ran on a scheduled route. These are not sense data but memories and suppositions; the most we can say is that they are memories of, or presuppositions about, sense data. So the empiricist who identifies experience with sensing must conclude that seeing buses is not part of our experience but a hypothetical construction more or less consciously based on our experience.

Dilthey agreed, indeed he insisted, that intellectual processes were involved in observing the world. But he considered it topsyturvy to imply that we start with the solid experience of sense data and, more tentatively, build up the world from it. It is misleading to think of perception as if it were a scientific investigation which starts from solid facts and then frames hypotheses about them. Dilthey thought it more natural to treat our sight of passing buses as the actual experience which is as reliable a basis of all our knowledge as we can get. Analysing this experience into components, such as data given by the senses and intellectual processes, is a secondary step.

Even talking about buses is usually a simplification. What we 'see' is the school bus taking the children from the housing estate to the junior school. Our observations of the life around us are obviously enriched by social and cultural knowledge; this, surely, is what we call experience if we are not influenced by speculative philosophic presuppositions; so this is where the philosopher must start taking the rich variety of life for his subject-matter, which he must analyse and interpret.

The fundamental idea of my philosophy [Dilthey wrote] is that no one, so far, has based his philosophizing on the full, unmutilated whole of experience, and so, on the whole fullness of reality. Speculation is certainly abstract. .... But empiricism is no less so. It bases itself on mutilated experience, distorted from the outset by an atomistic theoretical view of mental life ... no complete human being can be confined within this experience. (Vol. VIII, p.175)[10]

In case it should be thought that the question as to what is to be treated as experience is merely a quarrel about words, let us refer to a methodological principle which Dilthey derived from his conception of experience (and to which we shall return in its proper context). We can distinguish two fundamentally different methods of inquiry and explanation; one starts by picking out or presupposing elementary factors (such as atoms, cells or reflexes) and uses them as building blocks with which to reconstruct more complex reality; the other begins with the complex phenomenon before us (the magnetic field, the human eye or the whole human personality) and tries to disentangle its constituents. Though Dilthey stressed the importance of both procedures he considered that the latter had a very special role to play in the human studies. Neglect of this method has led to failure and lack of progress, for sometimes we cannot get back from the simple to the complex and so lose sight of the distinctive characteristics of the latter. It is doubtful, for example, if we shall ever be able to explain political decision in terms of such elementary processes as reflexes, learning by rote or simple inference. But we can certainly achieve something by analysing the complex products of political thought. In advocating that we should start from life, that is from unmutilated experience, Dilthey undoubtedly wanted to recommend the more extensive use of the latter method in the human studies.

After looking at Dilthey's negative view of metaphysics and his epistemology we must say something about his moral philosophy. We have already seen that for him a philosophy, if it is to be relevant to life, must provide guidance for our actions, i.e. it must help us to arrive at reliable principles of action. But we have also seen that he did not think that philosophic systems could deduce moral principles from their picture of reality, because that picture was not rationally justifiable. Experience cannot provide guidance either. It can show us what people think, feel or do and the consequences of their actions, but we need only reflect for a moment to know that there is a gulf between the conclusions drawn from such facts of experience and a moral judgment. Let us assume that we collect statistics as to how many people would like to be promiscuous or are promiscuous and enjoy it, and that to this we add information about the long-term effects of promiscuity: would this tell us if promiscuity is right or wrong? Being desired does not make it desirable, being enjoyed does not make it right, but causing suffering does not make it wrong, for telling the truth may also cause suffering and yet be right.

Dilthey knew this perfectly well, but he clung to the idea that there must be some connection between man's fundamental nature and his place in the universe on the one side and moral principles and ideals on the other. Man's rationality and social

55

nature are unvarying characteristics relevant to any morality, but it is equally important that man does not have an entirely fixed nature, and shapes himself in the course of his history. It is, in fact, a characteristic of human nature that man changes his nature by reflection. A product of mind, like the Christian religion, reflects some of the potentialities of human nature and at the same time moulds man in accordance with those it has selected. To summarize, Dilthey thought that moral principles could be deduced from facts but those of man's own intellectual history, not the hard facts of psychology or the behavioural sciences. So moral philosophy can give us guidance by critically examining and crystallizing our awareness of our own aspirations. Dilthey expressed this view in a letter to York (December 1892, pp.156–7). After mentioning the dangers of modern materialism he continues:

My book arose from the conviction that the independence of the human studies, the historical knowledge contained in them, could help to overcome this influence. Put differently: the historical world, once we reflect on it, encourages vigorous, spontaneous vitality and reveals an order *which cannot be formulated in thought* but which can be analytically shown *in individual life, in interaction*, and finally in a special higher order which transcends the scientific approach. If this order is to attain the elevated, confident, validity it once had it must be singled out and vigorously expressed.

He was trying, by studying history, to highlight the dynamic, spiritual forces at work in human life.

So we see that all of Dilthey's philosophic discussions converge on one theme; the study of man. For him philosophy in general aims at man's self awareness, epistemology is about man as a knowing subject and moral philosophy about man as a spiritual and socially active being. The constant emphasis on life means that we can only see the world from the human point of view and within the horizons of our own social and historical reality.

This knowledge of man comes to us through experience, though it only becomes explicit when the philosopher reflects on it. We gain some of this experience by introspection and the contacts of everyday life, but it would be one-sided if it were not extended by the findings of the human studies. So Dilthey asked himself how adequate and reliable these forms of experience were. How do we acquire our knowledge of human life when dealing with other men and studying history or society? Is such information trustworthy and what makes it so? Because he attributed great importance to these questions Dilthey embarked on a philosophy of the knowledge of man—a philosophy of the human studies—which is his most seminal achievement. This is my central theme, and other subjects such as his epistemology, his philosophy of language or his aesthetics will be drawn into this context, as they were by Dilthey himself.

5

The human studies

The idea of grouping together the different disciplines concerned with man and contrasting them with the sciences is particularly associated with Dilthey's name though it was not so much the idea as the conclusion he drew from it which was new.

His preoccupation with this topic from the very beginning of his career is not particularly surprising because in the nineteenth century the perennial interest in the study of man was stimulated by the challenge of social and political problems as well as by intellectual developments which acquired an impetus of their own. Historiography received a powerful impulse from the Romantic movement and its preoccupation with the past. The work of Hegel and, a little later, that of Marx and the so-called historical school gave intellectual backbone to the idea that history provided an important key to all problems. As a result history used its material more scientifically and extended its range to social, economic and cultural matters. There was renewed interest in philosophy and comparative jurisprudence, and economics, psychology, sociology, demography and social anthropology gradually emerged as independent disciplines with methods of their own. Important developments occurred in such spheres as the study of heredity and the theory of evolution which, though not belonging to the human studies, have a direct bearing on them.

This intellectual climate generated new problems leading to further developments in the human studies. The spectre of overpopulation conjured up by demographers forced attention on to the need for social control. Evolutionary theories appeared to challenge and undermine the traditional religious views of man's nature. Anthropologists discovered differences between human groups which suggested that man's nature was more flexible and more culturally determined than had been suspected. Psychologists appeared to debunk man by reducing even his higher activities to physiological processes which he shared with the lower animals. The historian's approach threatened the objectivity of all our beliefs and moral convictions by suggesting that they were relative to time, place and circumstances. Common to all these disciplines was the problem of their status and methodology; many of the practitioners of the human disciplines, when they looked at the progress the physical sciences had made since the sixteenth century, felt that the theoretical perfection and practical utility of their own work left much to be desired. So they asked themselves if the human disciplines could be made as systematic and reliable (in a word as 'scientific') as the physical sciences. This was followed by a second question: how important and fraught with consequences was the familiar, commonsense, distinction between the human studies and the sciences?

Dilthey shared his contemporaries' interest in these questions: when he classified all the disciplines under the two headings of *Naturwissenschaften* and *Geisteswissenschaften* he was only reproducing in German J.S. Mill's distinction between the physical and moral sciences. (Unfortunately we cannot simply return to these terms because 'moral sciences' has virtually gone out of use. The most commonly used equivalent is 'human studies'.) But what distinguished Dilthey from his contemporaries was that, instead of emphasizing the features which the physical and human disciplines had in common, he explored their differences in depth.

If we are to understand Dilthey's concept of *Geisteswissenschaften* properly, we must appreciate the precise meaning of the word. The second half raises few difficulties once we have reminded ourselves that *Wissenschaft* has a wider meaning than science. It embraces every type of scholarship so history and philology are normally described as *Wissenschaften*. *Geist* needs a fuller explanation. It is a common German word for which there is no adequate English equivalent. Moreover, by Dilthey's time it had acquired various nuances because of how it had been used by German philosophers, especially Hegel.

Geist can be translated as 'mind', 'spirit', 'ghost' or 'wit'.
'Ghost' and 'wit' do not help us in our study of Dilthey though
it is interesting to note that the German term is not quite so
solemn as translations sometimes imply. 'Spirit' is often the most
appropriate word in English, for example, in the 'spirit of an
age' and some translators have used it consistently. The drawback
of this policy is that 'spirit' suggests the higher aspects of the
mind. A Whitehall farce is as much a product of *Geist* as a
religious drama but to call it a 'spiritual creation' makes German
writers like Dilthey appear pompous. In most cases it is least
misleading to translate *Geist* by 'mind'. This gives it the neutral
meaning we want when we say that Shakespeare's plays and
slapstick comedies, Beethoven symphonies and 'Monopoly' are
all creations of mind. But even 'mind' does not match *Geist* in
every respect. *Geist* is used in the impersonal and general sense
of such phrases as 'mind over matter' but not when we refer to
individual minds. In such phrases as 'I can't make up my mind',
'Are you out of your mind!' or 'Two minds are better than one',
Germans do not use *Geist*. This qualification has to be remembered when 'mind' is used for *Geist*.

The difficulty is even more acute when we have to translate
geistig', the adjective formed from Geist, meaning what pertains
to mind. This cannot possibly be called 'mental' which means
'psychological' (even, possibly, 'deranged') for which the German
is *seelisch*. To obscure the difference between the two, would
falsify Dilthey's thought, because he quite deliberately replaced
seelisch by *geistig* in his manuscript of *The Nature of Philosophy*
in order to emphasize that he was concerned with the products
of mind and not psychological processes. So for *geistig* we must
use such phrases as 'created by mind' or 'mind-dependent'.
Geistige Welt becomes 'the world of mind' and *not* 'the mental
world'.

We can now attempt a positive account of what *Geist* means
in Dilthey's writings; basically it has two aspects. On the one
hand, it is the intellectual and creative capacity for abstract
thinking, conceptualizing and logical reasoning which distinguishes man from all other creatures. On the other, it describes
whatever is produced or shaped by the creative activity of mind.
Following Hegel, Dilthey called this latter aspect the *objektiver*

Geist ('objective mind') which consists of what he described as the *Objektivationen des Geistes* ('the objectifications of mind'). Languages, religions, codes of law and sciences, but also houses, gardens, tools, machines and ornaments are 'objects' of this kind.

The concept of objective mind, or the world of mind as he sometimes called it, plays a prominent part in Dilthey's philosophy of the human studies so it is important to understand it precisely. Dilthey himself, though he had taken the concept from Hegel, was anxious to give it a clear down-to-earth meaning which avoided any suggestion that it was a speculative idea about the nature of ultimate reality. As a convinced empiricist he insisted that it described entities within our experience. All the objectifications of mind are, like natural objects or processes, observable by the senses. We hear words and we see houses. But they differ from natural objects by being the products of the mental processes of human beings with which we are familiar—the thoughts, feelings or imaginings which go into writing a book or designing a garden.

So much is straightforward and requires little justification. Common sense accepts that there is a physical sphere (an outer world) and a sphere of mental processes (an inner world). It also accepts that thoughts can be expressed in physical gestures or applied to making tools. What is not equally obvious and needs explaining, if we are to appreciate the use Dilthey made of these Hegelian concepts, is the need to treat objective mind or the world of mind as a third, distinctive, sphere. His point is that we need this concept to describe facts and relationships with which we are also familiar but which escape conscious scrutiny if we do not pick them out by means of a common name. A book, for example, is not just paper with marks on it but contains ideas originally developed in the author's mind and recreated in that of the reader; but they are there in the book even when the author is dead and no one is reading it. Though a physical object without consciousness it has a mental content and can be described conveniently as an objectification of mind.

The same applies to numerous entities and their relationships to which we constantly refer. When I say that a full house ranks higher than a pair in poker, that Monday comes before Tuesday or that cat is *Katze* in German I am undoubtedly talking about

61

something, though it is neither a physical fact nor the mental states of particular people. These statements are true even when it is Friday and no one is playing poker or talking about cards. To call them relationships within the world of mind is only to recognize a distinction we normally make.

Dilthey thought it important to employ the concept of objective mind because it helped him to pinpoint the fact that the human studies must deal with relationships of people to the kind of entities which make up the world of mind. People are affected by religion and moulded by educational systems, they dedicate themselves to science or dodge the law. This is why, as Dilthey's terminology helps to remind us, the social sciences cannot confine themselves to human behaviour but must deal with such entities as ideologies or social systems which require a very different approach.

The English term which comes nearest in meaning to Dilthey's *objektiver Geist* is 'culture' as used by social anthropologists, but it has the disadvantage of obscuring the relationship between the mind as a creative force and objective mind which is its creation or manifestation.

If we take this explanation of what Dilthey meant by *Geist* as a guide we must conclude that the *Geisteswissenschaften* deal with man's intellectual powers and their products. This definition fits such disciplines as philosophy, comparative religion and literary criticism. It also excludes from the *Geisteswissenschaften* any study of man which is mainly concerned with his physical properties such as physiology or physical anthropology. By this definition the two groups of disciplines, the *Geisteswissenschaften* and the *Naturwissenschaften*, are neatly divided by their subject matter, the former dealing with *Geist*, the latter with nature. But Dilthey was not content with this division; because it excluded too much from the *Geisteswissenschaften*, he thought his own term misleading and introduced careful qualifications. His concept of *Geisteswissenschaften* was intended to represent the various studies of man, including history, psychology, economics, anthropology, sociology and politics. If men were disembodied and passionless intelligences these disciplines could be pure *Geisteswissenschaften* but, as they are not, the disciplines must deal with flesh and blood human beings and the situations in which they find themselves. This is why the translation 'human studies' catches the sense in which Dilthey used *Geisteswissenschaften*', as long as one does not lose sight of the concept of mind which is emphasized in the German. Dilthey's point is that the human world is not identical with the world of mind but is only truly human when permeated by mind. What distinguishes man from other creatures is that he is constantly involved in cultural contexts of his own creating. Even the direction his instincts take and the way he relates himself to other people are usually culturally determined and such purely physical features as skin colour become important because of the cultural prejudices and social responses they evoke.

Dilthey stressed the important role of mind in the human world in order to draw attention to the methodological problems it raised. He traced the development of the human studies and showed that in Antiquity and the Middle Ages the studies of man and society remained largely subservient to metaphysics and theology. In his own time he saw them becoming subservient to the more successful physical sciences, a tendency he felt he had to oppose. The human studies, he argued, could only profit from the example of the great pioneers of science like Galileo by imitating, not their actual methods, but the way they chose them to fit their subject-matter. So he thought the time had come to examine the whole methodology of the human studies and place it on firm foundations.

He asked what radical difference the involvement of mind made to the human world and picked out a number of the features which have no equivalent in nature. One of these is the purposiveness of human life. It is true that many religions and philosophies have treated the whole of nature as purposive. (The falling stone was thought to hasten towards its home on the earth, the egg to be bent on becoming a chicken, the acorn an oak tree and the whole of nature to serve a divine purpose.) But the modern science initiated by Galileo and his followers increasingly rejected any explanation in terms of purpose and had a cogent exponent in Spinoza. The idea of purpose lingers in biology but mostly in a metaphorical way—the bird builds its nest in order to lay its eggs and rear its young but we shrink from calling this its purpose. Even where the behaviour of higher animals appears most purposeful it is only a hypothesis that they have a purpose. There is no such question in the human world. Why am I putting on my shoes? I could answer in terms of nerves, brain cells and muscles, even of absentmindedness, but the answer which is normally given and expected is in terms of purpose. I am putting on my shoes because I intend to go for a walk. Explanations in terms of a purpose or intention appear unavoidable and it is hard to imagine historical, sociological or psychological accounts of human activities which do not use them. Indeed, the crucial process of understanding communications would be quite impossible if we could not presuppose that the sounds or signs which people produce serve a purpose.

Another feature due to the presence of mind in the human world is the making of valuations, based on the capacity which man shares with other creatures, to respond positively or negatively to the environment. But only man builds scales of value on this basis and makes judgments as to what is good, desirable, valuable, attractive, and what is not. Consequently we cannot discuss individuals or societies, everyday occurrences or historical events adequately without making various types of value judgments. The moment we call a man ambitious or dandified, describe a society as militarist or egalitarian, or refer to an action as shabby or altruistic we are making such judgments and, what is more, implying that the people we are talking about have made their own value judgments (i.e. a militarist society is by definition one which values military activity).

A third characteristic which mind imparts to human life is the role which norms, rules and principles play. They range from moral principles to traffic regulations, from rules of etiquette to by-laws about drinking. They are numerous and affect the methodology of the human studies materially, for they differ substantially from the laws used in science. The latter are generalizations based on observations; so, explaining the movement of a falling stone by the laws of physics, boils down to showing that this is what stones, given the particular circumstances, normally do. The laws—from the criminal code to traffic regulations—which human beings obey are conventional and changeable; they explain human behaviour only when people know about them and have chosen to accept them. This makes the two kinds of explanation in terms of law very different.

To this list of characteristics we must add the fact that human life is historical. Mindless nature, too, has its history; planets cool, an iron rod may break because it has been hammered for some time; trees grow and decay. But where consciousness and, with it, memory are present, the cumulative effect of successive events also affects our thinking. The strategy of the second world war was coloured by the fact that the leaders had tried—successfully or not—to learn the lessons of the first world war.

Because of our power to communicate with each other, personal recollection is augmented by historical records. We become heirs to traditions which determine what institutions we have, how we do things and why we believe one thing rather than another. The field mouse has, presumably, much the same sexual habits in different countries and these have not changed through the centuries. But courtship and marriage are not the same in Sweden and Pakistan and were different again in ancient Greece. This has at least two important consequences for the student of the human world. First, he has to use such general concepts as state, nation, marriage, family or capitalism with great circumspection, because what can be said about all the manifestations covered by one of these concepts may be extremely meagre. It may be more valuable to talk about the late medieval state, nineteenth-century capitalism or the family in modern Britain.

Because we are shaped by our traditions, the most appropriate explanation for social and historical phenomena is often itself historical. Why does Great Britain's Parliament consist of a House of Commons and a House of Lords? Why do more people live in southern England? Why has the cotton trade declined? In answering such questions one may have to refer to permanent human characteristics, to climate or geography and even to unchanging aspects of governing or trading; but a very important ingredient of any explanation must be a historical account of how the present circumstances were produced by a sequence of past events.

It must be clear that the different features listed by Dilthey are interconnected. Valuations, for instance, give rise to purposes and these, in turn, make us value the means for their achievement.

Values, principles and purposes are all subject to historical change and have to be explained historically. Dilthey thus showed how the world of mind differed from the physical world which is only purposive in an analogical sense and historical in a superficial way and which knows nothing of scales of values or of self-imposed principles.

Dilthey concluded that these differences made different methods of investigation in the human studies necessary. The physical world is there to see and touch, and observation provides the solid foundations of everything we know. Theories about the origins of these observable facts or the connections between them are only conjectures. The world of mind, on the other hand, is not directly observable; purposes, values and norms cannot be seen, nor can the subject-matter of history, because it lies in the past. Our knowledge of the world of mind comes from two sources; one is inner experience which makes us aware of purposes, values and norms, and reflects the past in the form of memories. Here the mind is at home among its own processes and creations, so reasons and motives, which are the equivalent in the world of mind of causal connections in the physical world, are directly accessible. Not only do we experience fear and the impulse to run away but we know how the one produces the other, an inner experience which puts us in direct touch with reality. An orange is only a phenomenon, something which, ultimately, may be different from what we see, but my anger *is* what I feel and not the appearance of something else. I know that it causes a certain action and need not frame hypotheses about the connection. The second source of our knowledge of the world of mind is communication, without which the individual's knowledge would be minimal. This involves observing the physical facts in which the world of mind is embodied and also requires that we should grasp a meaning that cannot be observed.

Once Dilthey had established to his own satisfaction that the world of mind had distinctive characteristics he was able to develop a philosophy of the human studies which could deal with their epistemological and methodological problems. So far, I have explained Dilthey's concept of the *Geisteswissenschaften* by discussing the meaning the term had for him, but it is equally important to consider the range of disciplines to which he applied it; he included a much larger and more catholic list of disciplines than is usually referred to by such commonly used terms as the humanities, the social sciences or the behavioural sciences. His concept of the human studies embraces economics, politics, sociology, anthropology, history, psychology, jurisprudence, literary scholarship and even philosophy, while we would, obviously, not dream of calling economics one of the humanities, philosophy a social science or literary criticism a behavioural science.

Dilthey's list of disciplines gives a fairly clear picture of what he meant by *Geisteswissenschaften* though he did not believe that it was complete or could be completed, because we can look at human life in innumerable ways. His intention in putting together what is divided in other classifications should be clear. He wanted to emphasize that all those disciplines are meaningfully related to each other. They have a common subject matter (though they may specialize in different aspects of it) and, consequently, the same cognitive processes are involved in all their methods. Finally, because they deal with different aspects of the same subject-matter, they are interdependent and can supplement each other. This vision of the inter-relatedness of all the disciplines concerned with man and his works reflected Dilthey's longing for a unitary vision and may provide a corrective to the present overwhelmingly strong drive towards extreme specialization; for today the quantity of knowledge and multiplicity of techniques virtually forces individual researchers to specialize not only in sociology but in the urban sociology of Northern England, not only in psychology but in the psychology of perception in retarded children.

Dilthey, however, was not content with a vague general idea of the interdependence of the different disciplines; he tried to show how they were actually related to each other. First of all, he divided the human studies into historical and systematic disciplines; then he picked out a number of specific disciplines to which he attributed a role crucial to the whole field of human studies; thirdly he divided the human studies into a number of sub-groups in terms of their special functions or area of study.

The distinction between historical and systematic disciplines is one of both goals and methods, though they may both deal with the same object. The various historical disciplines, such as political history, economic history, the history of ideas or the history of science (usually described as branches of the one subject history), try to tell a meaningful story in which individual objects and events and their relationships to each other are described and explained.

By systematic disciplines (or studies) Dilthey meant those, such as economics, sociology and psychology, which classify their subject-matter and explain it in terms of general laws. Economics, for instance, may deal with inflation in terms of generalizations about the relationships between factors that have formerly proved to be relevant; economic history may deal with the same subject, but in terms of its development in particular countries at particular times.

The historical and systematic disciplines are, according to Dilthey, interdependent *because* of their different approaches. The historian could not tell a coherent and meaningful story unless he recognized typical features in events and general laws in the way they are connected. That a general was afraid, and so retreated, makes sense to us because we have some general knowledge of human nature. i.e. we know the effect fear has on men. (The same applies to the interaction between physical and mental factors in the historical process. We are not surprised when a particularly muddy road delays a retreat because we know that heavy objects like gun carriages sink into soft ground.) So any historical account only makes sense in the light of almost innumerable generalizations, something we tend to ignore because many of them are familiar and trivial. The historian, who knows about the effects of anger or the results of mud without consulting psychologists or physicists, is hardly aware of engaging in an interdisciplinary project. But such common-sense knowledge is frequently not enough because we need more detailed and precise knowledge of complex facts than unskilled observation can provide, so the historian may have to rely on physics or chemistry or, more frequently, on psychology, sociology or economics.

The systematic disciplines in turn depend on history; broadly defined to include case-histories, biographies and other records, it provides the bulk of the empirical evidence on which all the generalizations of the systematic disciplines are based. Because human affairs are subject to historical change, only records, not generalized assumptions, can tell us what the family, the state or even human nature were like at a particular time.

Once again we observe the circularity of the interdependence between the historical and the systematic study of a subject. We can only be sure—to choose an example almost at random—that the economic situation of a country affects its political stability at a particular moment if someone has already established regular links between the two spheres of life. But how can we establish such links except by studying the effect of economic conditions on political life in particular instances? Economics and psychology must rely just as much on history, as it does on them. The recognition that this kind of circle is involved in the pursuit of knowledge, is, as we shall see, a characteristic feature of Dilthey's philosophy.[1]

The contrast between history and the systematic disciplines, based as it is on a fundamental difference in their aims and methods, is best described as a dichotomy of the human studies, but it could be seen as taking *one* discipline and giving it a special place, as Dilthey did with psychology. He argued—particularly in his writings of the 1890s[2]—that every sphere of life studied by the human disciplines arises from specific mental processes or experiences; at the heart of religion lies religious experience and economic life revolves around the desire to maximize profit. By analysing such mental states the psychologist can provide important clues for all other disciplines from history to literary criticism. In every case a circle is, once more, involved, for only by studying religion or economic life can we discover how the human mind works in these spheres.

Besides psychology he also picked out hermeneutics as a discipline of special importance for all the others. Though he sometimes stresses the key role of one and sometimes of the other at different stages of his career, it is, in my opinion, a mistake to think that he changed his mind and contradicted what he had said before. It is integral to his whole approach that, from different points of view, different disciplines appear to be the key discipline. Briefly, hermeneutics, about which I shall have more to say in Chapter 10, is the methodology of interpretation, which is so important because interpreting texts, or other manifestations of mind which resemble texts in conveying a meaning, is involved in all the human studies. Considering how we can do this effectively ·is,· therefore, a precondition of all research into the human world. But hermeneutics does not provide an absolute starting-point, because the principles of interpretation grow from its practice in different fields like law and literature.

Dilthey also tried to illuminate the relationships between disciplines by making various sub-divisions. One of these was the distinction between theoretical and practical disciplines which corresponds roughly to that between science and engineering, or physiology and medicine. Theoretical disciplines aim primarily at knowledge, practical ones at applying it methodically, though this distinction is, of course, not absolute. Theoretically orientated disciplines such as history may also be put to practical use and those designed for practical purposes, the study of law, for instance, may produce theoretical insights. Nevertheless, a fundamental difference in outlook and function remains. The psychology of perception is a theoretical discipline, educational psychology a practical one.

Another distinction which overlaps with that between theoretical and practical disciplines, but is by no means identical, is suggested by Dilthey's introduction of the concept of the disciplines about 'man in action'. These deal with the different ways in which human beings impose ideals, principles, purposes and rules on their wills. Law, politics, economics and educational theory are all examples of disciplines which deal with the role of norms or standards in our lives.

These various distinctions may give the impression of scholastic hair-splitting, but the way Dilthey developed and used them in his voluminous writings makes it clear that he was preoccupied—in a very practical way—with the different functions the human studies had to fulfil and how they could fulfil them. It must be particularly remembered that, in such fields as sociology, he was groping his way into as yet untrodden territory. He anticipated, for instance, distinctions within the subject-matter which have led to the development of different branches of sociology by contrasting cultural systems with systems of interaction. By culture he meant the cluster of beliefs, conventions, rules, institutions and social relations which make up the religion, science, art or literature of a community. By systems of interaction he was referring to the patterns of interlocking causal chains within a society which show, for example, the way in which social changes produce revolutionary situations that in turn affect cultural life. In Dilthey's hands concepts like these were intended as analytical tools for the study of complex social reality.

Perhaps oddest of all is Dilthey's inclusion of philosophy among the human studies. Nowadays it is usually considered different from all other disciplines because it does not try to arrive at factual knowledge. But Dilthey thought philosophy was man's attempt to discover himself, and so fulfilled the qualification of being a human study. Here is the point of substance behind what might otherwise be merely a matter of words—the close interdependence between philosophy and the empirical human studies.

Dilthey did not elaborate his various suggestions about the roles of the different human studies and their relations with each other to form a neat edifice, because he mistrusted rigid systems. Had he done so he would only have been overtaken by the developments which have since occurred in the field of the human studies. Disciplines that Dilthey discussed have acquired new aims, new terminologies and new specialisms; new subjects have been developed and the field of inquiry divided up in novel ways; fresh forms of cooperation have been pioneered. But this does not rob his broad framework of its fruitfulness.

His insistence on the need for an overall strategy to direct the cooperation between different specialists and disciplines is of lasting importance. He was convinced that such a strategy had to be guided by a general conception of man and aim at the consolidation and enrichment of this presupposed idea of human nature. This view of the human studies justifies and encourages recent developments in interdisciplinary cooperation, an idea on which he had many interesting things to say. He pointed to the interplay of psychological and social factors in the shaping of personality and stressed the need for cooperation between psychology and sociology; he demonstrated in his own research how literature could provide valuable material for psychologists, sociologists and historians, and explored how the law provides clues to human nature and social condition. He was deeply preoccupied with the development of a kind of psychology which could be of direct use to historians or students of politics. Above all, he never tired of insisting that the reliability and adequacy of the methods used by different disciplines could not be taken for granted and that their conclusions must be questioned and critically evaluated; so the results of the empirical human studies are neither final nor unambiguous, and interdisciplinary cooperation must include philosophic examination.

By grouping the various disciplines concerned with man and his doings together under one name, Dilthey stressed their interdependence. His name is—rightly—associated with this conception but, to dispel a possible misunderstanding it may be useful to anticipate a point which will be developed later. Dilthey's distinction between the human studies and the sciences is not intended to be absolute. Because man is a biological creature who lives in a physical environment the lines of interdependence, which make cooperation desirable, run across the frontiers of these groups of disciplines. History must take account of geographical factors, psychology of the physiological features of man, social anthropology of the findings of physical anthropology. Once this is recognized, it is only a matter of words whether we talk of cooperation between a human and a scientific discipline or consider psychology and anthropology single, but hybrid, disciplines. Dilthey himself was, undoubtedly, interested in the physical foundations of the human personality (the influence of man's speech organs on language, the role of man's upright posture in his development, and the mental changes which illness produced), but this side of his interest is less known because he did not produce any original work in this field. He did, however, produce the outlines of an intellectual framework—one might call it a philosophy of science—which embraces research into both the cultural and the physical worlds.

It remains true, however, that the differences rather than the affinities between the human studies and the sciences were the focal points of Dilthey's interest. Few thinkers in his lifetime doubted that the sciences could produce and, in fact, were producing genuine knowledge. Philosophers had accepted this assumption and carefully analyzed the reason for this confidence. Dilthey asked if the same could be said about the human studies. Were they able to tell us more about our fellow men than common sense and if so could philosophy justify this extra knowledge?

To answer such questions he directed his attention to the intellectual process or processes which distinguish the human studies from the sciences and which were, he believed, imposed on them by their subject-matter. This is why he considered it important to submit these processes to a searching epistemological analysis and to explore the way they are related to others in the human studies.

6

Understanding (*Verstehen*)

The concept of understanding as the intellectual process which gives us access to the human world, plays a crucial role in all Dilthey's work.[1] It almost became his trademark. Thanks to his influence it became a key concept in the disciplines known as *Verstehens-soziologie* ('Understanding-sociology') and *Verstehens-psychologie* ('Understanding psychology').[2] It is important, therefore, to get as clear an idea as possible of what he meant by understanding and why he considered it so crucial. His conviction of its importance rests on four assumptions; that understanding is a common process of everyday life; that it is important as a source of even the most elementary knowledge of human beings, let alone that of complex social matters; that it is a unique process, i.e. one which cannot be derived from or replaced by another; and, finally, that it is the one essential part of the methods of the human studies which differentiates them from the sciences. In this chapter we shall look at his reasons for these assumptions.

When we use the term 'understanding' we usually mean grasping what people say or write or, perhaps, convey by other means such as gestures or facial expressions. The German word *Verstehen* used by Dilthey has precisely the same meaning. Both words are equally vague or precise, and need just as much or as little clarification. There seems little reason for leaving it untranslated as some commentators on Dilthey have done. This simply fosters the unjustifiable idea that we are dealing with a somewhat strange and mysterious concept rooted in uniquely Germanic

74

ways of thinking and, therefore, small wonder that scholars have complained of the difficulty and obscurity of the idea.

Philosophers have often used the term 'understanding' in the same way as ordinary people. Hobbes, in *The Leviathan*, refers to 'Ignorance of the signification of words which is want of understanding . . .' So there is nothing odd or revolutionary about Dilthey's using the word in the same way. But philosophers, to avoid the looseness and ambiguities of common usage, have to be a little more precise than people in everyday conversation. It is neither safe to assume that philosophers faithfully reflect every vagary of common speech nor wise to complain if they do not. The only safe way is to observe closely how a philosopher himself specifies his terms. In Dilthey's case common, but subsidiary, uses of the term 'understanding' have given rise to some misunderstandings. One is to argue that he must have used 'understanding' for any type of comprehension, even that of physical relationships, because it is one of the proper uses of the term (as in 'he understands the working of steam engines'). All one can reply is that Dilthey made it clear that he did not use the term in this way. Had he done so, he would have been flatly contradicting his claim that understanding plays a special role in the human world.

Another misunderstanding encouraged by reliance on everyday use is the identification of understanding with sympathy. Husbands proverbially complaining that their wives do not understand them are assumed to be grumbling about their partners' emotional response rather than their intellectual grasp. Dilthey's own writings occasionally encourage the idea that he used 'understanding' in this sense and thus based his whole approach to the human studies on feeling for and with other people. It is tempting to think that Dilthey, influenced by the Romantic movement, produced a Romantic theory of emotional involvement with others, for he discussed sympathy and empathy and their relevance to understanding at some length. But if one considers his work as a whole and weighs the implications of his approach, it is clear beyond question that he thought of understanding as an intellectual and not an emotional process. Understanding what people say obviously covers '2 plus 2 is 4' or 'open the window' as well as the complex web of propositions which makes up

Plato's philosophy or the American Constitution. By no stretch of the imagination could sympathy be the central feature in understanding them. In some cases of course sympathy helps, but where and to what extent this is the case remains a purely empirical question. If someone tells me about his grief, can I understand him better because I, too, loved the man whose death he mourns, or because I have suffered a similar loss? These are matters for inquiry but they do not touch the common core of all understanding.

It should also be noted that, for the sake of brevity, I shall speak of 'understanding' or 'the process of understanding' in this book where it would be idiomatic to refer to 'trying to understand' or 'the process of gaining understanding'. The context will make it clear if the term is used to describe an achievement, or to denote the process leading up to it for which there is no single word in English.

Understanding is as ordinary and familiar as seeing, remembering, imagining or reasoning. It is an essential part of Dilthey's case that, like all the other basic cognitive processes, it is part of everyday human life. It is not a specialized technique, not something invented by philosophers or devised by social scientists. It is as commonplace as hearing or touching things. Friends greet us, signposts point the way, posters announce a concert, and we understand them as a matter of course. Though we make mistakes we would consider somebody mad if he doubted that we are all, even the mentally dull, capable of such understanding. This capacity is no more or less mysterious than any other normal aspect of human life. Nor does it involve intuition or inspired imagination though they may be needed to do something exceptionally well or in a very difficult case. Understanding Plato, like preparing a superb meal, requires exceptional gifts. Understanding 'Good morning' and boiling an egg do not.

The fact that understanding is familiar makes it of special interest to the philosopher. His job is not to discover or explain new and unheard of things but to explore the hidden presuppositions of what we take for granted because it is a part of normal life. It was because understanding is such an ordinary process that Dilthey put so much energy into examining the grounds on which we can claim that it is a *valid* cognitive process.

Understanding is not only ordinary and familiar, it is also pervasive and fundamental. Without it human life is inconceivable. Cooperation at work, the education of children, harmony in the home, social life and political institutions all depend on mutual understanding. By this I do not mean emotional accord or bonds of sympathy, but people grasping what is said and so not talking past each other. Where sympathy is also required we depend in no small measure on the success of verbal communication. Because this is well appreciated it has become a commonplace to blame many of our contemporary problems, such as industrial unrest or juvenile deliquency, on failures of communication.

Understanding what people communicate to us is so important for everyday life and to the human studies because man's capacity to develop and use complex systems of languages, to talk and write, send messages by morse or signal with flags, is his most striking feature, distinguishing him from everything else in the universe and making history and civilisation, law, morality, art and science possible. Metals and flowers do not communicate with the investigator; they can only be observed and examined. Even animals only communicate in an elementary way which we interpret or misinterpret in terms of human analogies. But, in the case of man, observation of his physical features and overt behaviour can only be a part, and indeed a very small part, of a comprehensive study. We must focus our attention on what people say or convey in any other way, try to understand what they mean and then we can understand *them*.

The human studies rely to a large extent on verbal material—oral or written responses to tests, questionnaries or interviews, eyewitness accounts, records of transactions, minutes of meetings, legal documents, inscriptions and literary works used by psychologists, historians, economists and sociologists—which explains the need for understanding. Just as doctors, unlike vets, listen to what their patients say, the practitioners of the human studies are in direct or indirect communication with their subject-matter.

Having established that understanding is familiar and yet very important Dilthey went on to show that this cornerstone of the human studies was unique, that it could not be derived from, or replaced by any other cognitive process. For if understanding did not differ from, or could be translated into, other processes, they would be the ones which would have to be treated as fundamental to the human studies. Basically there are two logical ways to challenge the unique place of understanding. One is to claim that it is used outside the human studies and is therefore not peculiar to them; the other is to deny that it is required even in the human studies. The first is largely a matter of historical interest, the second very much one of continued debate.

Few people today claim seriously that understanding—in the sense used by Dilthey—is a universal process though the idea is deeply ingrained in our thinking. Because the experience of living and communicating with other human beings is universal and intimately familiar man, for long periods of history (and, indeed, prehistory), tended to look at nature anthropomorphically and to think of most knowledge as derived from communication. Earth and stars, rivers and trees, animals and birds were thought to be inhabited by spirits resembling men who could speak and reveal their secrets. Even recent poetry reflects this view. Poets tell us, without appearing crazy or ridiculous, that the brook babbles, the reeds whisper and the thunder speaks. Indeed, some metaphors introduce this conception into everyday speech. We talk of the sea beckoning or the sky threatening.

Though Christianity put a damper on the idea of nature being animated by spirits, it gave rise to an alternative conception which also suggested that knowledge was received by communication. The universe was seen as the divine text which man tries to decipher. The pioneers of modern science found that talking about the book of nature eased the transition from reliance on texts to reliance on observation.

If any of these versions were true all knowledge would, indeed, be a matter of understanding. Knowledge of nature would differ from knowledge of the human world only because understanding of a different kind of language was needed. As a historian of ideas Dilthey was interested in this whole approach but did not feel that it presented a serious challenge to his theories. The other alternative, that of denying the need for understanding as a distinctive intellectual process, is still very much to be reckoned with. Indeed this case and, with it, the attack on Dilthey's position has been further developed since his death. It is, therefore, well to consider its strength in terms of Dilthey's explicit or implicit arguments against it.

The attempt to eliminate or, at least, devalue understanding is part of the revolution of thought which produced the triumph of modern science in the seventeenth-century. The philosophers and scientists who pioneered this movement emphasized the importance of knowledge derived from perception and considered all other kinds of knowing derivative, marginal and of doubtful value. Descartes supported this new trend by making it very clear that, as sources of knowledge and education, history and literature were inferior to mathematics and science. Spinoza, though he mentioned the matter only in passing, went straight to the crux of the matter. He distinguished perceptual knowledge from knowledge gained by hearsay and then, in a single sentence, lumped them together as what he called 'the first kind of knowledge' because he considered the difference between them trivial. Essentially his point is this: seeing a flowerpot and being told that there is a flowerpot on the table, provides the same information, but the second source of knowledge is inferior and derivative because it depends on the speaker having seen the flowerpot and the listener knowing, from his own experience, what seeing a flowerpot is like. Thus communication does not generate, it only spreads, knowledge which, in the process, may be diluted or distorted. Understanding providing only secondhand knowledge is, therefore, parasitic. Due to the influence of these two great philosophers, subsequent theories of knowledge tended to concentrate on perception as the model source of reliable knowledge.

This philosophic view, and the methodology of science erected on its foundations, presented students of the human word with a clear message; that it was desirable to eliminate the need for understanding in the human sphere just as it had been eliminated in the physical. If the babbling brook or even God's voice is not needed as a source of information, perhaps we need not listen to people either. These attempts to by-pass understanding have usually gone under such names as positivism or behaviourism. I shall consider briefly three typical examples of the way they argue.

One approach is to concentrate entirely on man's physical features and observable behaviour and submit them to the same processes—such as classification and statistical analysis—as the physical sciences. What does not lend itself to such treatment is ignored as irrelevant. This has made it possible to achieve accurate and reliable results but they are often trivial and useless because too much has been left out. It does not look as if this method has made much progress in explaining some of the more complex phenomena of human life. That the investigator's own activities, such as classifying and analysing statistical data, cannot be accounted for in the terms chosen by him is obviously damaging to this whole line of approach.

Another way of eliminating understanding is to try to translate it into behavioural terms. The idea that understanding means grasping what someone conveys about his own state of mind is rejected. Instead, understanding is defined as the observation of certain correlations between behavioural acts which allow us to expect one type of act to be followed by another. For instance, understanding, 'I am hungry', is taken to mean that a person uttering these sounds can be expected to eat when given food. This means that there is nothing special about understanding; it is just like expecting thunder when you have seen lightning. To assume that anything more is involved is condemned as sheer mystification. However, it is easy to demonstrate the inadequacy of this theory. There are innumerable ways of conveying that one is hungry. It can be said in different languages, it can be written or indicated by signs. If, then, one asks what a sequence of signs on paper has in common with, let us say, pointing to one's stomach the answer in terms of the behaviour we observe, must be 'Nothing'. Even the suggestion that they are *followed* by the same behaviour will not stand up to scrutiny. A person who says he is hungry may not eat the proferred food for a thousand reasons. He may be slimming or his religion may forbid it. The only thing the different forms of communication have in common is shared meaning. Before we can group these different forms of behaviour together we must have understood their meaning; so the whole theory collapses.

The third way of getting rid of understanding as a serious issue has been a matter of practice rather than theory. A good many social scientists appear to act on the assumption that, though understanding obviously occurs, it can be taken for granted as trivial and unproblematic. This view presupposes that understanding is generally, and automatically, successful in producing an undistorted picture of what is referred to. It is like a pair of spectacles which we can ignore because we are sure that they do not distort, affect, colour or magnify. We can simply turn to the objects as if they were directly in front of us. On this assumption a good deal of research in the social sciences seems to imply that people who say they like brand X or admire politician Y are brand X users or supporters of Y. This is the source of some spectacular failures by opinion polls and market research investigations. After all, it does not need much knowledge or imagination to envisage how much misunderstanding both of questions and answers, how much lying, teasing or self-deception, can intervene between words and facts. The theory of the transparency of language, as we may call it, only needs stating explicitly to reveal its absurdity.

The futility of these attempts to eliminate understanding from the centre of the human studies demonstrates better than long theoretical arguments how irreplaceable it is. Having established this Dilthey had to consider how such an everyday process enters into and affects the methods of the human studies.

It may be well, at the outset, to be clear what we mean by a method. Generally speaking, it is a systematic arrangement of procedures designed for a purpose which, in the kind of method we are talking about, is the acquisition of knowledge. It should be absolutely clear by now that understanding itself is not a method; conceived as a process it can be one ingredient of a method and, as an achievement, it may be the result of using a method. So, what we are concerned with is the relationship between different procedures and our question at the moment is how the characteristics of understanding influence these relationships. From Dilthey's writing we can extract three conclusions which have a bearing on this. First, the process of understanding is already complex and its different aspects link it to different contexts. Secondly, it is interdependent with various other processes and, finally, it combines with, and colours, the cognitive processes which the human studies share with the sciences.

By expanding on the structural complexity of even simple cases of understanding we not only throw light on Dilthey's methodology but also supplement the original definition of understanding. Acts of understanding have, basically, three aspects, each of which can be emphasized by a different definition. Defining understanding as the grasping of what people say or write draws attention to the outward process, the pervasive fact of human life—that people talk to each other and comprehend the words or signs thus exchanged. It is equally important to define understanding as the comprehension of meaning and so draw attention to the fact that we must understand the ideas or feelings which expressions express. As we read Darwin's master piece for example, and understand the words, we come to understand the theory of evolution. Understanding must, thirdly, be defined as entering into people's minds, whether in the trivial sense of appreciating that they are greeting us or in the deeper sense of sharing their intimate thoughts or feelings.

These three aspects of understanding are inextricably linked and interdependent. We cannot understand words or signs without understanding their meaning and hence something of the speaker's mind. Put the other way, we cannot understand a person without grasping what he has to say or comprehend what he means without taking in his words. Yet the three definitions given above reflect distinguishable aspects and are, therefore, far from equivalent. It is perfectly possible for a person to understand every word said to him and yet be puzzled about the speaker's intention ('What is he going on about?'). It is equally possible to be clear as to what is in someone's mind without understanding his words properly ('He is obviously begging.').

Dilthey emphasized one or the other of these conceptions in different works and at different stages of his career. This does not mean that he was confused or had changed his mind, only that his focus of interest had shifted. In his biographical writings he was clearly concerned with the relation of a work to its author's experiences, thoughts and creative processes. As a philosopher of history he stressed the importance of close textual study and the use of philosophy. As a student of philosophic and literary works he emphasized how the meaning of texts (or other manifestations) could be revealed by scrutinising their structure and relations to wider contexts.

But, if it is true that his various interests influenced the aspect of understanding he stressed at any particular time, it is probably equally true that he extended his interests so widely over so many fields because he wanted to explore the different aspects of understanding systematically one after the other.

Keeping the three definitions of understanding and their relation to each other in mind is worth while not only because they reflect Dilthey's wide-ranging and yet closely interrelated interests but also because they protect us from various misunderstandings. Understanding people may, for instance, be mistakenly thought to be intuitive if we do not remember that it is based on the familiar process of grasping what people say. Similarly, apprehending meaning may be confused with revelation if we forget the link with the other definitions.

From the point of view of methodology this triad of definitions is especially valuable because it specifies the different directions interest may take even in everyday understanding and how these are related to each other. One person may read Dickens' novels to learn English, a second to get a picture of nineteenth-century England and a third to study Dickens' mind. Even the ordinary reader, who has no other purpose than to enjoy himself, may be specially attracted by the style, the story or the author's attitude. Philologists, literary critics, psychologists or social historians may study the same work, each from his own point of view and *with his own purpose* in mind. Yet none of them can achieve his aim unless he can rely, to some extent at least, on the success of the others. One cannot understand Dickens' picture of English life without understanding the words he uses. (Here even an Englishman may need expert help where the meaning of words has changed since Dickens' time.) But it may be equally impossible to understand the words without understanding something of the life of the time described. For instance, we may only appreciate the reference to a particular farm tool if we know something about the agriculture of that period. However, the overlap is only partial. Though they are all dealing with the same text, each specialist will relate it to a particular context. The linguist will compare it with other works of the time, the psychologist with other information about Dickens' personality and the social historian with other accounts of the period. It should be clear, even from this simple illustration, that this conception provides a highly suggestive model of how different disciplines are related and can cooperate with each other to their mutual advantage.

From these relationships between different aspects of understanding we can pass to those between understanding and other cognitive processes. Here, too, we find that knowledge depends on cooperation. Perhaps no case is more illuminating than that of perception. We have already seen that understanding is an independent process in the sense that it cannot be identified with, or replaced by, any process such as perception, but this does not mean that understanding is independent in the sense of being able to operate without it. Much of what is said to us can only be understood because it refers to what we ourselves can perceive. Moreover, words or gestures must themselves be perceived. Up to this point Dilthey agreed with the behaviourists that the study of man must start from and be rooted in observation of his behaviour. (He, of course, disagreed with them that this was all, or even the most important part, of what the student of humanity can do.)

This dependence of understanding on perception does not give the former a subsidiary status because the dependence is mutual. To show this we need only pose a very simple question. How do I know that I really perceive something and am not suffering from an illusion or hallucination? Clearly, by comparing my impressions with those of others or, at the very least, my own earlier ones. So we have to understand what others say or what we have recorded in the past. In this sense, all the physical sciences also rest on a basis of understanding and would be impossible without it.

There are many and various intellectual processes which are similarly related to understanding. There is no need to go through a long list because a single illustration will make the point. The process of comparing is quite distinct from understanding but it is very often required by it. How could I conclude that my friend is peeved because he greets me rather coldly, if I could not compare his greeting with previous ones? Such comparisons, in turn, depend on our ability to understand concepts. (I assume that this is involved when I compare what I see now with what I recall having seen yesterday.)

This web of interdependencies is already involved in the apparently simple acts of ordinary understanding in everyday life. We can easily and automatically perform the numerous acts of perceiving, remembering and comparing involved in understanding that someone is saying 'good morning' but saying it rather coolly. We consider such processes highly reliable and scepticism would seem eccentric. But the moment we pass from such simple cases to more complex ones, from a greeting to, let us say, a legal clause, a religious ritual or a political manifesto, the position is completely changed. We can no longer be confident of success in understanding them and must consider what processes we can use and how to apply them. In this way the question of method arises even in the more complicated cases of everyday life. It becomes even more critical when we pass to the systematic study of man in the human disciplines.

A methodology is not an instrument by which we can churn out discoveries. There is no substitute for imagination, intelligence and patience. But methodology may help the researcher to reflect on the lessons learned in the past. In other words, once some ingenious research has proved successful it is possible to discover and formalize some of the steps which made it so. As a result, one can list processes, such as the framing and testing of hypotheses, which are necessary if reliable knowledge is to be gained and one can even prescribe the proper order in which they should occur.

One methodological issue in the human studies is the relation between more and less complex acts of understanding. So Dilthey analysed the way in which complex understanding was achieved by relating numerous acts of elementary understanding. To understand a Shakespeare play or a treaty between states we must not only understand the individual words or the motives of individual characters, but also the ways in which they are related to each other. Beside these acts of understanding of various complexity other intellectual processes are also involved in the cognitive methods of the human studies (or, for that matter, in everyday knowledge of human life). In sociology as much as in

85

physics, in literary interpretation as much as in chemistry, practitioners generalize, frame hypotheses, compare and make deductions. So the relationship between understanding and these other processes raises further methodological issues.

There is nothing very controversial about my description so far but I am preparing to make a point which is not quite so obvious and on which Dilthey has been misunderstood. It is this: understanding, combined in various ways with other cognitive processes, is involved *at every stage* of an investigation within the human studies. It is, emphatically, not something which can be confined to a special role, like providing hypotheses or explaining results.

A simple illustration may clarify this point. Let us assume that we are dealing with a study of the way people shop in supermarkets. To start with, understanding is required even before the basic situation is in front of the research worker. If he only sees moving bodies and hears noises shattering the air there is no human subject-matter for him to study. It is only when he can take in what people say, discover the aims pursued by the shoppers and read the signs in the shop that he has found his subject. The early stages of an investigation, such as classifying the evidence or comparing different cases, involve understanding as well. It would be futile, for instance, to classify shoppers simply according to the quantity they had bought. What they buy and whether they are influenced by advertising may be of interest. Equally interesting may be the way they differ in their reasons for buying; some may be buying from impulse, others from fear of shortages and others again according to a regular plan. Little would come from an investigation which lumped these different activities together as if they were the same; they can only be differentiated if we can understand them. Once we have grouped our samples and are ready to devise an explanatory hypothesis further understanding is necessary. Even before we can ask the shoppers questions which might help us to discover why people give rein to their impulses in supermarkets, we must have some idea as to how people are likely to be motivated. When, finally, we test whatever hypothesis we may have framed, we must understand what is said in response to our questions.

Though this is neither a full nor a realistic account of a

scientific investigation it should indicate the view Dilthey took on this matter. Understanding must combine with different cognitive processes but pervades the social scientist's whole approach. It is neither an initial stage of commonsense assessment which will be left behind once the scientific process is properly under way, nor just a final goal to be pursued by other means.

This is as much as needs to be said at the moment about the role of understanding in Dilthey's methodology; but as the subject of understanding is woven into his whole philosophy it will become much clearer when two related topics have been discussed. One of these is the nature of the entities—the words and signals—on which understanding has to operate. The other, which figures prominently in Dilthey's thought and requires discussion, is meaning. When these have been dealt with we can consider the foundations on which understanding rests in the wider context of Dilthey's whole theory of knowledge.

7

Expressions

'Every little movement has a meaning all its own'. These are not Dilthey's words but those of a song which accompanied a dance routine in a British TV Spectacular (Maclean show). But they might well have been his for he was convinced that human beings express their thoughts and feelings, observations and purposes in more ways than we realise. They use language—the most important human characteristic—but not only language; consciously or unconsciously, deliberately or by accident, they convey their meaning in gestures, grimaces, actions, even by their choice of clothes. (Indeed the ladies of the chorus were not referring to movements of the vocal chords or of a hand guiding a pen.) Literature and art, social life, the course of history and other objectifications of mind all reflect, and so reveal, the human mind.[1]

The existence of these expressions in such abundance and variety makes human life knowable. 'For', as Dilthey wrote, 'man does not understand himself through some kind of introspective brooding which only gives rise to the great Nietzschean misery of exaggerated subjectivity. It is only by understanding the historical reality which he has produced that man becomes conscious of his power for good and evil' (Vol. III, p.210).[2] He put it even more succinctly in his last writings. 'Life is not revealed to us directly but illuminated by the objectifications of mind' (Vol. V, p.LX).[3]

Men come to know each other, and even themselves, only by understanding their own and each others' expressions. There is more than a grain of truth in the quip, 'How do I know what

I think, until I hear what I say?'. Information about others depends even more obviously on what they say or do. What is true of ordinary life applies equally to the disciplines concerned with man. The only material they have to work on are expressions. It is their range which defines the limits of the human studies.

This range of expressions is there for all to use. Anyone who thinks that he must concentrate and rely on only one type of approach, such as laboratory experiment, for his knowledge of man is like an observer who peeps through the key-hole when the door is wide open. Dilthey was the last to deny the value of psychological experiment but he insisted that we must also use the evidence of history and literature, of law and art.

Because he believed that expressions were the main source of our knowledge about man Dilthey asked himself *how* they could be used in research. To answer his question he had to make clear what their main features were and distinguish different types of expressions so that he could evaluate the merits and demerits of each. However, he did not confine himself to these necessary but fairly straightforward clarifications. He also explored, in an interesting way, the whole subject of expressions in terms of one particular class—namely literary expressions. Dilthey's different observations about expressions amount to a coherent theory which underlies all his work. The elements of this theory are scattered through his works and must be brought together.

One of the universal, defining, characteristics of all expressions is that they mean something, i.e. represent or refer to something other than themselves. It is part of their nature that we not only look at them but beyond at what they point to. Only when we stop looking at the extended finger and follow the direction in which it points can we understand that we are confronted by an expression; then we can begin to understand its meaning. Nothing is more familiar than the relationship between expressions and what they express. But because it is unique it cannot be explained in terms of other relationships such as similarity, temporal succession or causal connection. The only thing one can do is to expand on some of the terms, such as meaning, employed in the definition of expressions. I shall take up some of Dilthey's points on this in the next chapter.

Because expressions are entities referring beyond themselves they have a curious double nature which distinguishes them from purely physical or mental objects. They are physical things or events which convey a mental content. This is the only way of defining expressions so as to distinguish them from non-expressive behaviour and physical objects which carry no message. A smile is not just a movement of the lips but reflects and communicates pleasure. A text is not just a collection of marks on paper but may take us into the realms of philosophy. Dilthey sometimes talked of this relationship in terms of inner and outer because it corresponded to the relationship between man's inner—i.e. mental—life and his outer behaviour. This of course is only a metaphor because the mind is not in the body, nor the joy in the smile, as a nut is in its shell.

From these universal characteristics let us turn to others which most, but not all, expressions share. The exceptions will become clearer when we turn to Dilthey's classification of expressions. One of these characteristics is that expressions tend to occur in contexts or are parts of configurations which define their meaning as well as the meaning to which they contribute. Words contribute to and are partly defined by the meaning of the sentence in which they occur. A smile is part of a person's whole demeanour and must be interpreted accordingly. Physical objects are also determined by their relations to each other but this feature is particularly important in the use of expressions. A pebble is much the same whether it lies on the beach or on the dining room table, but a word acquires a different significance according to the place in which it is spoken or the context in which it occurs.

Expressions are, also, purposive. The only exception is behaviour such as blushing or trembling which Dilthey classed with expressions because it reveals a person's state of mind. Apart from this we can, normally, only recognize a sound, a movement, a mark on paper, or a piece of material waving in the wind as an expression when we are satisfied that it results from purposive action (though the purpose is not necessarily to communicate). This is the principle behind, for example, Freud's famous heuristic assumption that apparently unintended behaviour, like mistakes or slips of the tongue, can be treated as meaningful expressions because they are the products of hidden or unconscious purposes.

To conclude the list of general characteristics we must mention that they are usually conventional and so governed by rules. This is most obvious in the case of languages, ceremonial greetings and rituals but can also be observed in the unwritten rules which prescribe that people should not laugh at funerals or yawn at lectures.

We get a fuller, more down-to-earth, view of Dilthey's conception of expressions when we see what he included under this term. In his main classification expressions embrace three distinct types of human behaviour: the use of language, bodily expressions and actions. It is not difficult to characterize each of these classes and distinguish it from the others. But Dilthey is making an important point when he groups them together. He is arguing that we can understand actions and involuntary gestures just as much, and the same way, as we understand words. They are all expressions and *together* constitute the source material of the human studies.

Under language he included not only languages like German or English but also subsidiary systems of signs such as algebra, semaphore or morse. Because, together, they play such a prominent part in our lives, Dilthey treated understanding them as an exemplary case of understanding. They have all the characteristics we have listed but are specially marked by the high degree to which they are governed by complex systems of rules and by the extent to which they can convey, through their complex structures, a variety of intricate meanings, fulfil various functions and achieve great precision. Dilthey did not produce a detailed philosophy of language, nor did he require one for his purposes. An outline of such a philosophy can, however, be reconstructed from the various scattered reflections to which we shall return in the next chapter.

Bodily expressions is the most accurate term for Dilthey's second class of expressions, though the literal translation would be 'expressions of life'. By these he meant the whole range of facial expressions, gestures, postures, the tone of the voice, and spontaneous acts, such as smiles, winks, cries of horror and sagging shoulders. Dilthey believed that, by their smiles or waves, their tears or hesitations, intentionally or unintentionally, people reveal not only their conscious thoughts and feelings but even mental states they had been unaware of. 'The small area of conscious life', he wrote, 'rises like an island from inaccessible depths. But expression lifts something from out of these depths' (Vol. VIII, p.220).[4] In other words, Dilthey formulated a theory of the unconscious, accessible only through its expressions, which anticipated, and provided a framework for, such theories as those of Freud and his successors. Since Dilthey's time we have become familiar with many such approaches to different areas of human behaviour; theories as to what hand-movements, doodles, slips of the tongue, stammering, sleep-postures and ways of sitting or standing reveal about personality have multiplied and, at times, even appeared in popular magazines.

In one respect the term bodily expression is inadequate. It does not indicate sufficiently that there are other means by which a person presents a picture of himself to others. The choice of hairstyle or clothes, perfumes and cosmetics, even a car or house, convey the same kind of information as gestures or postures. People do not wear their clothes only for protection from the weather or comb their hair so that it does not fall over their eyes. These choices usually reveal, and are frequently intended to reveal, something about the person, such as his social status, his role in society, sexual availability or character as a citizen.

Expressions of this type are not as invariably governed by rules and conventions as language. Blushing is so little under our control that it cannot be subjected to conventions. Laughter or tears may often be beyond our control yet they have been conventionalized to some extent. We are expected to laugh at our host's jokes. Because it was acceptable for Homeric heroes, but not for Victorian gentlemen, to weep in public, their tears had a very different significance. The choice of clothes and hairstyles is largely conventional (including certain conventions of being 'unconventional'), so are types of bodily movements; for example the supposedly characteristic behaviour of homosexuals, so often parodied by comics, is, in fact, an imitation of how ladies of fashion moved in the 'twenties.

Dilthey's third class of expressions covers actions. What chiefly characterizes them is that they are purposeful behaviour though their main purpose is not communication. Usually we walk out of a room because we want to be somewhere else or use a hammer because we want to drive in a nail, though occasionally we may use such acts as a kind of language; for instance, leaving a room to show that we are annoyed, or swinging a hammer to demonstrate how busy we are. But Dilthey wanted to stress what common sense acknowledges when it says that 'actions speak louder than words'. He considered that actions *were* expressions because, though they differ from the other expressions in that they do not necessarily intend to convey anything, they do reveal something of their author's mental life, i.e. his purpose. A politician who is campaigning hard manifestly wants to be elected. A man sawing away at a tree wants to cut it in half. These intentions must not be confused with motives about which Dilthey was much more sceptical. A politician may run for office for many reasons—money, power or prestige—and his actions may not make clear which of these motivates him (indeed he may not know himself). Dilthey stressed this point because he thought that historians and social scientists became unduly discouraged when they failed to pass from discoverable goals to elusive motives.

Some simple actions may be largely determined by a person's desires and his assessment of the circumstances but the majority are also governed by rules and conventions, so, without knowing these, we can not understand the actions. This is as true of ballroom dancing as of plumbing, of waging war as fishing for trout. If we see a brewer performing some particular operation we only know what he is doing if we know something about the established ways of making beer.

Beside this main classification into language, action and bodily expressions Dilthey also used some cross classifications which emphasize the kind of distinctions we have already mentioned. Expressions may be natural or conventional, though the former may be relatively rare in the human world. They may be intentional or not, though the latter may only occur marginally. Even if expressions are intentional they may, or may not, intend to communicate. Indeed, these two features may be combined in a complex expression in such a way that they can be classified differently according to the researcher's point of view. For instance, a man's conversation may intentionally convey his view on foreign policy but it may also show—much against his will—his vanity or lack of humour.

Dilthey made a further distinction between simple and complex expressions, between, let us say, a wolf whistle and a symphony, a swear word and a philosophic thesis. All we need to remember is that an expression may be composed of many simpler ones. Finally, Dilthey distinguished transitory from permanent expressions—by and large a distinction between human acts or bodily expressions and the products of such acts. Smiles, cries of pain, derisive gestures and the spoken word are transitory books, films, photographs, diaries, letters, as well as buildings and gardens, tools and weapons permanent.

Three further characteristics of expressions must be discussed in order to appreciate Dilthey's approach properly. They are creativeness, adequacy and effectiveness, and differ from those previously discussed by being distinctly 'good' qualities. In other words, we approve or disapprove of expressions according to whether they have more or less of these characteristics. Though this applies to different types of expressions it is particularly relevant to linguistic ones because they play such a crucial role in our emotional, intellectual and cultural life, so I shall concentrate on the way Dilthey applied his views to words.

Expressions are creative because they do not merely represent or reflect how we perceive a situation but add something new. We have already come across one way in which this occurs. Expressions lift something from unconscious depths. It may be that I only become aware of being afraid when I see my hands trembling, so the expression itself has changed the situation for me. When we turn specifically to linguistic expressions we find that they contribute to the situations they describe in many ways. The terms we use provide us with concepts which structure our experience. For example, when I say that I have seen a lion I am not simply referring to a set of sensations because I automatically relate what I see to all kinds of ideas about lions including, perhaps, the idea that they are powerful and dangerous. It is this general idea that I remember and may be able to convey to others while I may not even have noticed such details as the animal's exact size and colour. Scientific knowledge, the superstitions of my community, my own past experiences and my own fantasies have defined the term 'lion' for me and this, in turn, determines what I see.

Man's capacity to form ideas or images by selecting from his experiences, then interpreting his present and anticipating his future in terms of these ideas, we usually call imagination. It plays a significant part in our knowledge of the world and was therefore of interest to Dilthey and to many philosophers before him. For several reasons he concentrated particularly on the imagination of poets.

The role of language is even more important and creative in the human sphere than it is in the physical where attaching a label may be crucial in making a situation what it is. If I call a situation humiliating it does humiliate me. If I think of what I feel about a person as 'love' I have gone some way towards loving him. If I speak of a man as a nigger I do not merely reflect, but help to create, a gulf between us. This process is familiar enough and is frequently referred to, in one of its forms, as giving a dog a bad name.

This may be familiar but it is also important, as Dilthey and the sociologoists who followed him recognized. The fact that human beings are conditioned not only by situations, but also by what they think the situations are, is part of our freedom. If we were only affected by circumstances as chemicals are affected by heat or plants by water we would be like automata. Instead we are affected by what we think situations are, by what they look like to us. If Dilthey had been talking only of such cases as staying at home because one thinks it's cold outside the matter would be trivial. Where what is said can easily be checked it is likely to be true and so there will be little difference in practice between being guided by one's opinion or by the facts. But Dilthey wanted us to recognize that we see the whole of reality in terms of our philosophy and religion, our scientific theories, and even in terms of the plays we have seen or the books we have read; in short, that we see it through the spectacle of our whole intellectual climate. This view of reality cannot be shattered or corrected by putting one's head out of the window and is, therefore, all the more pervasive and powerful. What really makes us free is that this view of the world which guides our action is our own creation.

But while Dilthey believed that expressions were creative and could never be mere replicas of reality he also recognized that those which were supposed to be descriptive had to be adequate representations. He believed that reality contained structures, characteristics and distinctions which exercise a constant pressure on the concepts by which we refer to them. He did not think that we could simply compare our idea of a lion with what we see, because perception, undistorted by any conception, is impossible. But he did believe that we can be aware, and even examine critically, how far a concept *fits* our impressions. To abandon this belief would lead to the fantastic conclusion that the world is whatever we chose to think that it is. We are perfectly familiar with the experience of looking for the right word to describe a situation or struggling to convey what we really feel in a letter. We are also well aware of the trouble taken by scholars and scientists to choose accurate terms and make adequate distinctions. So, expressions are required to be adequate and we can judge them accordingly.

But expressions have other functions than that of representing the reality they refer to. They are intended to convince, persuade, entice, stimulate or incite those who hear or see them. Naturally we require them to do this as well as possible; in other words, we are concerned with their effectiveness.

The three features of expressions (of words in particular) which we have listed play a decisive role in human life. Our creative picture of the world colours our whole outlook, the adequacy with which we can represent reality determines how successfully we can cope with things and the effectiveness with which we can communicate governs our social relations.

From these conclusions it is easy to deduce how important literary works are for human life. They are, after all, specially designed to be creative, adequate and effective. This is what makes them so influential in society and so instructive for the social scientist trying to understand it. For this reason Dilthey's literary studies and aesthetic theories form an integral part of his philosophy of the human studies (though undoubtedly he also studied them because they satisfied his aesthetic sensitivity and abiding love of poetry).

The poet, endeavouring to use language creatively, adequately and effectively, is doing something we are all concerned with in our lives, but he is doing it methodically, and for its own sake, what we do more casually and for practical reasons. The good poet also does well what we do fumblingly. In this way he lights up reality for us freshly, clearly and forcefully.

Dilthey's approach becomes even clearer if we pursue a little further his point that the poet's job is not purely formal, not simply to say prettily what can be said plainly. Undoubtedly formal characteristics, such as rhythms, rhymes and the use of sonorous words, play a part in making poetry adequate and effective. These are not only conventional decorations; the form of a poem can give emphasis where required and what Dilthey called its 'verbal music' creates a mood which enhances the meaning of the words. But this is not all; no poem is an objective, though apt, description, for the image it creates superimposes the poet's feelings and interpretations on what he sees. Eliot's *Waste Land* is not a photograph of our world but a fresh way of seeing it. Some of the images created by literature become widely accepted ways of looking at particular experiences and even enter every-day speech. Coleridge's albatross tied round the sailor's neck is such an image. Catch 22 is a more recent example. So a successful literary work has three important aspects: it interprets its subject matter creatively, it reflects and reveals what is true about it and, by spelling out its vision in words, it provides us with the means of thinking and talking about the subject.

The problems of interpreting, depicting and conveying experiences are often tackled in a consistent way by individuals or communities and so they develop their own style. Though the idea of style is usually applied to artistic expressions such as literature, painting and architecture, it can, according to Dilthey, be extended to nearly every sphere of life because most human behaviour is expressive; so we speak of styles of dressing and eating and even of styles of life. It often makes sense to speak of the styles of nations, civilizations or ages, by which we mean their common way of thinking, feeling and choosing and how they express them.

So far we have discussed the general characteristics Dilthey attributed to expressions, the way he classified them into language, bodily expressions and actions, and then used such distinctions as those between natural and conventional, fleeting and permanent, to produce cross classifications. Finally we turned to his account of the creative and persuasive uses of expressions and their application in literature. Dilthey made these detailed points about expressions because, for him, they were the basis of our knowledge of the human world. Let us now turn to his purpose when he classified expressions and brought out their different characteristics—namely to assess their value for research. His examination of the methodological implications of these differences between expressions was integral to his whole approach.

Different types of expressions have different advantages and drawbacks. Linguistic expressions have the enormous advantages that they can be very full and explicit, informative and precise; they can convey many details and nuances. Their drawbacks as a source material of the human studies were, according to Dilthey, that they can be quite impersonal (i.e. a book on rock formations may tell you little about its author), that they can easily be used to deceive and that understanding them depends so extensively on rules and conventions that they may easily be misread.

Bodily expressions are much less structured than languages and cannot convey such complicated messages but they have compensating advantages. 'Events of our inner life which we have not thought about', Dilthey wrote, "are dredged, as it were, from the depths of the mind by bodily expression. Such expressions spring directly and spontaneously from the mind and so become definite objects which can be understood; they contain, therefore, more personal experience than introspection can discover" (Vol. VII, p.328).[5] What Dilthey meant is that a person may, for example, recoil from a spider and only then become aware that he is afraid of these creatures. Such expressions have the marvellous power of revealing hidden recesses of the mind and, moreover, exposing the truth, because being spontaneous they cannot be easily faked.

Dilthey thought that the great advantage of actions was that they usually show clearly the goal to which they are directed and give some indication of what the person doing them is like. But actions, too, have their limitations as sources of knowledge; not only can people act deviously; even more important is the general fact, which Dilthey stressed, that actions are partly determined by circumstances and may thus not reveal, or may even misrepresent, their author's nature and motives. We understand clearly enough when someone says that he is afraid. We may gather the same thing when we see him trembling and turning pale. But can we draw the same conclusion when we see a general beating a retreat? Not at all; it is only when we know such factors as the lie of the land, the strength of the opposing forces or the instructions he has received that we can judge if he acted from fear or not.

The expressions we normally have to deal with are conventional, for not only words but also most bodily expressions and actions are governed by conventions. When we know the conventions we have often gone a long way towards understanding the expressions; indeed, in simple cases the convention *is* the explanation. (He smiled because he was expected to do so in greeting his guests and that may be all there is to understand.) Understanding an expression—once we know the convention— can be precise and reliable. But this great advantage is balanced by the incomprehension to which ignorance of the conventions condemns us. We cannot know that some people raise their clenched fists in greeting rather than as a threat until we have learned their convention. Natural expressions do not suffer from this drawback. We can recognize a friendly smile, a gesture suggesting we should stand back or a caress without the aid of conventions. They have the great advantage of providing fundamental and direct contacts between human beings and for these there is no substitute because they can link people of entirely different cultures. They are also the foundations on which we build when learning our mother tongue. How else could a baby get started except by learning to associate words with his mother's smiles, caresses or pointing finger? The drawback of natural expressions—which include some bodily expressions and some spontaneous actions—is that they are relatively rare. We have already noted that even such things as smiles which *can* be spontaneous and natural can also be conventional. Their other disadvantage is that they are relatively crude and do not allow for such complex communication as conventional expressions.

Continuing with Dilthey's list of classifications we come next to his division into expressions which are intended to communicate something and those which are not. The former are methodologically important for Dilthey, because he thought that we could not possibly appreciate other people's points of view, their conceptions of the world and ideals of life without understanding what they want to convey. Expressions of this kind are readily accessible because most people are willing or even eager to put their own point of view, to say what they think or feel. Such expressions are also sometimes very explicit because some people are extremely articulate. On the other hand what people unintentionally reveal in their words, bodily movements and actions is, by comparison, fragmentary and obscure. But these expressions have the inestimable advantage that they are free from the deception or self-deception which often distort deliberate communications.

The methodological implications of classifying expressions into simple and complex are obvious. Those which are simple can be easily and reliably interpreted while the complex ones reflect the intricacies of human life. It is also clear that complex expressions may have to be interpreted in terms of the simpler ones of which they are made up and simple ones in terms of the complex ones of which they are part. But Dilthey added a qualification which is highly characteristic of his approach. He emphasized that we cannot fully reconstruct and completely understand complex expressions in terms of the simple ones of which they consist but must confront complex ones directly.

The implications of the distinction between fleeting and permanent expressions, too, are straightforward enough. Smiles or waves or the tone of voice have an immediate impact. They are vivid and rich in allusive overtones. This is their value. But they are only accessible to those present at a particular moment. Once gone they cannot easily be recaptured because eye-witness accounts, films, tapes and photographs often distort what they try to retain. Permanent expressions, such as books or buildings, have the advantage that they can be inspected repeatedly and studied at leisure. They are accessible to any number of investigators who can compare their impressions and check their conclusions. This is why Dilthey thought that the human studies had their best chance of being objective when they used this type of material systematically. Man comes to know himself mainly by using this indirect route. As we have seen, Dilthey called these expressions the objectifications of mind and their sum total, objective mind. This is why he called the disciplines concerned with man 'the studies of mind'. But these expressions have their drawbacks too. They can be relatively remote from those who created them and so we must take intervening factors into account, which makes interpretation more difficult; for example, to evaluate an eye-witness' account we need some independent information about any bias he may have. The same is true if we want to know how far a novel reflects the author's attitude and how far public taste. Houses and gardens can only speak clearly of their creators' preferences when we know what material they had to work with.

It should have become clear that Dilthey's various classifications divide the whole field of expressions from different points of view so that the same expressions figure in different classifications each designed to bring out a particular contrast between characteristics. Just as we classify a person as male, a catholic and a white collar worker so we classify an expression as conventional, fleeting, and an action. When a research worker tries to judge how reliable and illuminating a particular expression is he must keep the methodological implications of all its characteristics in mind. In the case of very complex expressions these may even be contradictory. A speech, for instance, is a conventional, deliberate and complex expression while a blush is natural, unintended and relatively simple; but when a person blushes while speaking we have a complex expression with all these conflicting characteristics. In fact, a complex expression like a speech may be classified under any one of the main types of expressions; it just depends on the aspect we emphasize. It is, clearly, a verbal act designed to communicate some information or instruction. Because the accompanying blush or the tone of the voice reveals—without the speaker's intention—something of his feelings, the speech may be treated as what we have called a bodily expression. It may also be considered as an action if it is intended to achieve a particular effect such as ending a partnership or sealing a pact. Only when we have analysed an expression from all these angles can we evaluate its usefulness as source material.

Different disciplines have, to some extent, different kinds of expressions as their main subject-matter; different investigations in one discipline may even use different types of material. History, for instance, relies largely on conventional and permanent expressions while psychology frequently takes account of natural and fleeting expressions. Within psychology we use different expressions according to whether we are studying perception or prejudice. In the light of these distinctions we can examine the methodological problems of each discipline or investigation.

It would, however, be a mistake to attribute to Dilthey the idea that expressions can be neatly parcelled out as belonging to particular disciplines. On the contrary, he insisted that the same expression may be of interest to different disciplines according to the point of view from which we look at it. Expressions may, therefore, be treated as points of intersection between disciplines. A speech—to keep to the original illustration—may be of interest to political scientists because it is part of an election campaign. If it makes the value of the pound fall it may also concern economists. Insofar as it is also the manifestation of a person's fears or ambitions it is a proper subject for psychologists.

To stress these points today is not superfluous. We still tend to talk as if certain types of expressions—delinquency, for example—were the sole preserve of one discipline which alone can explain it completely. However, just as we may only be able to appreciate the political importance of a speech when we have assessed its economic impact, so we may only be able to explain the psychological aspects of the delinquent when we have assessed the social reasons for his crimes. If Dilthey's analysis is right, interdisciplinary cooperation is much more than something desirable but inessential; it is an indispensible condition of any major piece of research.

There is an even more important issue on which Dilthey's comprehensive and commonsense view of expressions provide a much needed corrective. Contemporary intellectuals are beset by two, opposite, forms of naive credulity. One is the belief that everything is as it seems; the other that nothing is as it seems. The first is seen most clearly in those eager researchers who solemnly question housewives about the washing-up liquid they prefer, the party they would vote for, or even the details of their sex lives. They go away and submit the data they have collected to statistical analysis and produce reports which may bring ruin to detergent firms, deceive political parties about their chances, and startle the reader with the extravagancies of suburban sex. The man in the street cannot be expected to be less credulous. He appears to accept the advice of the confidence-inspiring people he sees on TV or hoardings without realizing that it is being given by actors. Dilthey points us to evidence which could correct such simplicity. There are usually signs that the lady being questioned on her door-step may only want to get rid of her tormentor as quickly as possible, to please, to boast or appear respectable. We know the actors telling us to use brand X are chosen for their ability to act which means that they can pretend convincingly.

Another form of credulity is the uncritical belief in one fashionable theory or another (for example, Freudianism) which maintains that we should disbelieve what people say about their aims and motives because they are apt to lie or deceive themselves. Human beings, such theories claim (and the claim has been widely accepted), are governed by hidden motives such as infantile sex or aggression; whatever they may think or say to the contrary is only a mask or defence-mechanism. I have heard a commentator on TV solemnly say that all of us in our hearts would like to smash pottery. What evidence, other than a general theory of aggression, could he possibly have? It would be quite idle to protest that one has never been aware of such a desire. In the same way various sexual tendencies are attributed to public figures. It is not particularly interesting to be told that a well-known poet is a homosexual, for we can learn much more about his true feelings from his poetry; the assertion may also be ill-supported. 'Where is the evidence?', we say, 'after all he was, by all accounts, happily married, did not have prolonged friendships with men and did not hang about public conveniences.' 'Ah' we are told, 'he was a *suppressed* homosexual.'

Another fashionable theory which encourages its adherents to ignore what is before their noses and look beneath the surface is Marxist inspired. How far the adherents of this theory have read and understood Marx is neither here nor there; it is obvious that they respond to novels, films or social changes in terms of the class struggle as predictably as Pavlov's dogs salivated at the sound of a gong.

The great virtue of Dilthey's approach to expressions is that it corrects such bias. People, he reminds us, express themselves in many ways and on many levels and *all* are relevant to the understanding of man's behaviour. It is unsafe to accept what people say without looking for possible evidence that they are lying or deceived about their own hidden motives, and unwise to ignore what is manifestly in a person's mind.

Artistic expressions played a special role in Dilthey's methodology. He narrowed his interest down to literary expressions because they could convey meaning more fully and richly than any other. Indeed, he thought that we needed language to understand any other type of expression. Michelangelo's statues, for instance, cannot be fully appreciated in purely sculptural terms but only when they are related to Renaissance thought and literature.

Literary works, apart from giving special aesthetic satisfaction, fulfil the same functions as other expressions but tend to do it better. The poet reveals and illuminates reality and, because he reflects in tranquility and uses words without any of the practical purpose which speech usually serves, often conveys truth more reliably than other observers of human life. So he throws light on both the unchanging features of human nature and the historical changes in society. Literary works crystallize and spell out more forcefully than everyday expressions the ideas, valuations and purposes dimly perceived by society at large. They are the mirrors of the age and, as they add something to the values and purposes they describe, are creative and provide new ways of seeing reality, talking about it and so changing it. So literature records what men and societies are like, educates us and helps us to shape our view of the world.

One can illustrate the different points of view from which

Dilthey used literary sources by glancing at his various studies of Goethe's work. One of these approaches was psychological but was not confined to the question of what Germany's greatest poet was like as a person. Dilthey thought that by studying Geothe's poetry and self analysis he could throw light on the processes involved in poetic creation. But this was not all; he believed that if an analysis of Goethe's imagination could illustrate the working of poetic imagination in general it could also show how imagination functions in all of us. By selecting a man whose imagination was powerful and forcefully expressed in an accessible form he could study human nature under a magnifying glass as it were. Dilthey applied this approach to other aspects of Goethe's mental life, for instance the way he saw the pattern of his life as an orderly progression.

Goethe's work was also source material for Dilthey the historian. In his early writings one can trace the rebellious spirit which, at that time, was overturning society in France; in his later works there is something of the resignation and concern with personal culture of an increasingly prosperous but politically powerless bourgeoisie.

Most striking of all was Dilthey's analysis of the way in which Goethe, together with some of his fellow poets, created the world-view dominant among the educated classes of ninteenth-century Germany. It was Dilthey's contention that Goethe's poetry successfully communicated a new sense of life and new ideals of personal conduct.[6]

So the poet's expressions take their place among other expressions as material for psychologists, sociologists and historians. Indeed, they are particularly important because they are articulate and influential. They also differ from other expressions *because* they are artistic. This means that they must be understood and evaluated aesthetically before they can be used by other disciplines. For instance a poet's expressions of his feelings may mislead a psychologist unless he knows that they are part of a poetic convention. Such information may make the expression particularly interesting to the historian of ideas. Aesthetics may be defined as the study of the principles which govern the adequacy and effectiveness of expressions while literary criticism is more specifically concerned with both the form and content of literary works. It aims to help the reader understand and appreciate the poem or play. This is just as necessary for the scientific use as for the full personal enjoyment of such works.

The help we need to *understand* literary works does not differ in principle from that required for any other kind of understanding. We must know the rules and conventions which govern the expressions and learn about the contexts to which they belong. In the case of a poem the rules may be those which govern the construction of a sonnet and the contexts may range from the poet's own interests to the circumstances of his time.

Evaluating literary works is equally necessary but raises much trickier points. To explain why valuations are necessary before the social scientist can use literary expressions, we may find the analogy with using witnesses in a court helpful. Some witnesses are observant, clear, truthful and objective, others are not. This does not mean that a court could, or would wish, to use only the first kind of witness. The lies and evasions of one witness can be just as revealing as the truthful statements of another. But this is only so if we can distinguish between them, i.e. judge their respective merits. This point must be made if we are to appreciate the role which Dilthey assigned to literary criticism within the body of the human studies (though he does not explain it himself). All kinds of literature are of interest to the social scientist but he must know the qualities of his witnesses. The critic must tell him how powerful the poet's intellect is, how acute his observation, how precise his expressions and how honest his interpretation.

If this evaluation is to be more than a purely hypothetical requirement it must be possible to evaluate literary works fairly. Here Dilthey had to argue a highly controversial point. It is an old saying that we cannot argue about taste, and many philosophers have discounted the possibility of making aesthetic judgements rationally and objectively. Dilthey's specific problem was this. Like most modern thinkers, he could not accept that reason by itself could provide objective standards of excellence and, all his life, fought the kind of eighteenth-century rationalism which believed this possible. On the other hand, he found a logical difficulty in deriving norms from experience. The latter tells us what things are, not what they ought to be. Modern philosophy, by and large, has stressed that the gulf between 'is' and 'ought' is unbridgeable so that the one cannot be derived from the other. Facts, like attendance figures or the loudness of an audience's laughter, tell us how popular a play is, not if it is good, which is something quite different and requires the application of standards. No value judgement can be derived from the fact that more people have seen *The Mousetrap* than *Murder in the Cathedral*. Dilthey's problem was to find a way in which reason and experience could support each other as a basis for norms. He relied, mainly, on two lines of argument.

The first is that once we have discovered a purpose we can use experience and rational arguments to establish objectively how it can be most effectively served. Then we can judge how well a particular object serves the purpose; this is how we decide what makes a pair of good walking shoes. All literary works can be judged in terms of how adequately they fulfil the general purpose of all literature, namely to communicate thoughts and feelings. A more precise judgment becomes possible once we have established the particular purpose of a literary work (to arouse a horror of war perhaps). This is one sense in which we can establish norms of goodness.

Dilthey's second line of argument concerns the more difficult case of judging the content rather than the form of literary works. Like many, though not all, literary critics Dilthey believed that we can only evaluate a literary work properly by discussing what it says and judging if it is important, true and inspiring or merely trivial. His conclusion as to how we can do this followed the lines of his theory about moral values. Values and norms, the products of our traditions, can be found by examining them. All we can do, if we are asked, for example, to justify the value of freedom (and therefore its greatness as a literary theme) is to point to the fact that philosophers and poets have pleaded for it and that men have fought and died for it. But these are not ordinary facts because we are not talking about statistics. A critical assessment is necessary because what matters is the quality of the arguments in favour of freedom and the actions on its behalf. Here, once again, we see the circularity so characteristic of Dilthey's thought. The literary scholar must himself unearth and examine the evidence for the standards he uses in his examination. An analogous circle is involved in the need for cooperation between literary scholar and philosopher. The scholar provides material for the philosopher's critical reflection, the philosopher clarifies the norms which the critic must use in his work, so each is dependent on the other.

The way Dilthey actually evaluated and used literature can only be appreciated properly when one reads his many articles and essays, his books and lectures in this subject, but I hope enough has been said to supplement his general theory of expressions. The study of literature and the use of literary criticism were so important to Dilthey because he thought poetic expressions were particularly creative, adequate, effective and truthful expressions. They are, however, only one aspect of the general expressiveness of life and so Dilthey attempted to classify them comprehensively and evaluate them according to their methodological importance. To take the subject a stage further we must next look at another important term of Dilthey's philosophy—'meaning', which is, what expressions are intended to convey.

8

Meaning

Meaning is one of the key concepts of Dilthey's philosophy; it is what expressions express and understanding understands. We have seen that what makes expressions meaningful is that they point beyond themselves to something else. A cry is meaningful when it reveals someone's pain, a word because it represents an idea. This is well-trodden ground and as Dilthey did not expand on it we need not do so either. But Dilthey did not confine himself to the meaning of expressions. He was at his most interesting when he considered another sense of meaning and how it arose.

One cannot properly appreciate Dilthey's whole philosophy without considering the striking way in which he placed his theory of linguistic meaning into the wider context of his theories about non-linguistic meaning, such as the meaning of actions, situations and of life in general. We use meaning in the latter sense as often as in the former but the ingredient which gives expressions their meaning is absent here. When we talk about the meaning of life or the meaning of historical events we are not suggesting that either refers to something outside itself. Indeed, Dilthey never tired of insisting that life 'does not mean something else' (Vol VII, p.234)[1] and describes it as one of the ruling impulses of his life 'to understand life in its own terms'.

This sense of meaning is as familiar as the other and we readily understand what someone wants to convey if he says that music means a lot to him or that he wonders what a particular event means. We know the speaker finds something valuable, interesting, important, relevant or significant, but is there a good reason for these two different uses of the same word? One could easily avoid any ambiguity by using interest or importance for the second sense, and so introduce a precise terminology. Dilthey did this at times by using the term *Bedeutsamkeit* ('significance') in contrast to *Bedeutung* ('meaning'), but he was not very consistent because he was, as even his closest disciples complained, notoriously careless in his terminology.

However, there was more than carelessness involved in Dilthey's use of meaning in both senses; he thought that to eliminate the idea that the two senses belonged together was to sweep important issues under the carpet and that the relationship between the two merited the closest philosophic attention.

Dilthey's theory of non-linguistic meanings and its relation to linguistic meaning is not only important within the context of his own approach but makes points relevant to current debates. First of all, by talking about the meaning of life, of actions and situations, he stressed the need to examine our basic human problems rationally.

There is always the danger that philosophers who confine meaning to language consider these wider issues 'meaningless' and, therefore, dismiss moral, political and cultural problems as unworthy of, or inaccessible to, philosophic examination. Finding answers to such problems must be left to preachers, politicians, public relations men and perhaps psychologists and sociologists. Dilthey's philosophy of life was opposed to such a view and, in his theory of meaning, he attacks it at its roots.

This theory neatly maps out the areas with which the social sciences are specifically concerned. Students of sociology will know that Max Weber and his followers singled out the subject-matter of sociology from the scientific study of mere behaviour (whether of human beings or of gases and metals) by focussing attention on meaningful action or just 'action' (already defined as conscious and purposive behaviour). Equally familiar to social scientists will be the idea that it is not situations and circumstances, but the meaning they have for us, which determines our actions. We react to the world according to the way we interpret it, feel its effect upon us and relate it to our interests and needs. Students of the human world also talk about the meaning of institutions and organizations when they discuss the role these play or the functions they fulfil in human life. By showing how actions, situations or institutions are all, though in different ways, meaningful, Dilthey pointed out the need for an overall framework for the human studies and for different approaches to the various disciplines.

The third area in which the value of Dilthey's approach can be illustrated is that of linguistic theory. Theories of language not based on a wider theory of meaning often appear incoherent and paradoxical.[2] There is, for instance, something absurd about treating the origins of language as *purely* conventional and underlining this point by speaking about language games. No doubt important aspects of language are entertainingly emphasized by this metaphor. The rules of grammar, like those of chess, have been conventionally defined, can be changed by convention, and govern what can or cannot be done. In both cases the rules are enforced by a single sanction: if you disobey them you have stopped talking English or playing chess. But, helpful though this analogy is, it makes, if pressed too far, a mystery of how language could originate or be taught, for one cannot pass on a convention without already being able to communicate. We saw in the previous chapter that Dilthey solved this problem by his appeal to natural expressions, but the force of his solution depends on the way he looked beyond expressions to the source of their meaning.

Many theoreticians of language have been more or less aware of this problem and have introduced assumptions about human life into their theories. But this has often been done in a casual, almost absentminded fashion. Dilthey tried to deal with it systematically.

A first rough introduction to his theory of non-linguistic meaning can be provided by a homely example. Dilthey himself kept his philosophic writings close to everyday experience. If I said that my last visit to Germany meant a lot to me and was asked why, all of the following would be appropriate. It was most enjoyable, it helped me with my research, it changed my view about German politics, it earned me some money, it gave me the opportunity of affecting the decision of the committee I attended, it renewed and cemented old friendships, it is part of my job. In other words the meaning of the trip is determined by

111

such factors as the way it affected my feelings, thinking and life, related to my purposes and fitted in with my expectations.

In general terms Dilthey's view is that meaning arises from man's involvement in his world. 'The meaning or significance of life' arose, according to him, either from 'the causal nexus in which what is valuable in life is produced or from the relationship of our satisfaction-seeking self to the external world' (quoted by Misch from Vol. VIII). Dilthey is even more explicit about the way in which circumstances become meaningful both by affecting us directly and by arousing our feelings (an illness, let us say, making us both weak and anxious).

We obtain pleasure partly from the nature of objects, their beauty or significance, partly from the way they stimulate our existence and personalities and so enhance our lives. This double relationship is rooted in the interaction between ourselves and the external world. Just as we experience outer reality through our sensations so we experience value, meaning and the stimulation or deadening of our inner or outer life, through our feelings (Vol. VI, p.150).[3]

Because such relationships are involved he thought it misleading to talk about *the.* meaning of anything (as we have done loosely so far). To speak of the meaning of life, of history, of a situation or an action is to adopt the kind of dogmatic and rigid view held by philosophers, priests or researchers which Dilthey emphatically rejected. There are only the meanings which individuals or groups discover in, or attribute to, life or history. On the other hand, attribution of meaning is not purely subjective and arbitrary like a whim or impulse. It reflects both an actual situation and the way it is grasped by a particular consciousness. 'The meaning of life', he wrote, 'lies in the way in which the parts of a person's life and the value he attributes to them are seen as a unit. This unity lies in the nature of life; it is meaning which is a category, derived from life itself' (Vol. VI, p.319).[4] Some ways of grasping meaning are common to us all because they are based on common human features; some are peculiar to groups, civilizations or societies (for instance, an agricultural community finds the changes of the seasons more meaningful than city dwellers) and some are not shared at all. Today may mean something to me, and to me only, because it is my birthday.

Dilthey pursued this concept that man's involvement in his world made his life meaningful into greater depth:

The basis of our consciousness of self is the abiding fact that without a world we would not have such a consciousness, and without this consciousness no world would exist for us. What occurs in this contact is life not a theoretical process; it is what we call an experience, that is, pressure and counter-pressure, expanding towards things which in turn respond, a vital power within and around us which is experienced in pleasure and pain, in fear and hope, in grief over burdens which cannot be shifted, in delight over what we receive as gifts from outside. So the I is not a spectator who sits in front of the world's stage, but is involved in actions and counteractions in which the same actualities are overwhelmingly experienced whether kings figure in them or fools and clowns. This is why no philosopher could ever persuade those involved that everything was appearance or show and not reality. (*Nachlass*, C32, Vol. II, p.335).

So experience is not merely awareness of mental images; if it were, we could, indeed, think of ourselves as spectators at a show. Instead we are involved as participants because what we experience helps or hinders us, causes us pleasure or pain. This, and not theoretical arguments, gives us the assurance that we are confronting reality.

In the above quotation the idea of experiences making up experience in general was made clear. There is no special term in English for the German word *Erlebnis* which Dilthey used frequently as one of his key terms. It corresponds to the sense in which 'experience' is used when we say something was 'quite an experience', meaning it affected us personally and was not just part of an impersonal flow of events. Where 'an experience' or 'experiences' are used in this book that is the meaning I want to convey.

'An experience', in Dilthey's own definition, 'is part of the course of a life in its total, concrete, reality from which nothing has been taken away; seen teleologically it is already a unity and contains past and future in the consciousness of the present' (Vol. VII, p.134).[5] Confronting a savage dog, for instance, is such an experience. It has a unitary meaning and becomes part of the history of my life. It is a combination of perceptions, thoughts,

113

feelings and desires enriched by memories and anticipations. It would not have been the same experience if I had not already learned about savage dogs in the past and had not anticipated his attack.

Experiences as units of meaning stand in larger contexts which contribute to their meaning and are modified by them. (They resemble words in this respect.) But, far from each being confined to one context, they figure in several simultaneously and so become crossing-points of the contexts. One of these is our knowledge of the external world which is built up from our separate experiences. A man's life is another context into which individual experiences fit. Dilthey described it vividly as a constant flow in which the future becomes the present and the present the past. But this flow does not affect the identity of individual experiences. Each retains a unity of its own in which awareness of the past, the present and the future are meaningfully linked. One is tempted, therefore, to liken the sequence of experiences to beads in a necklace. Dilthey himself described the way experiences are related in time as follows. 'The qualitatively determined reality which makes up our experience is a structural context; it occurs in time and is experienced as a sequence: temporal relationships within it can be grasped but whatever, though past, continues to influence the context or sequence in the present *is* present in this respect' (Vol. VI, p.315).[6] This technical sounding point is really quite simple. Being attacked by a savage dog can be described as an experience though it consists of a succession of events—the dog's growling, crouching and springing—of which I am aware. If I am then terrified it is not because the dog is jumping at me but because he is doing so after he has growled. Dilthey thought he had to underline these familiar relationships because they constitute the meaning of the whole experience.

Dilthey then turned to some of the significant ways in which experiences can be related in a person's life. It is obvious that all of them follow each other in time but it is worth noting, as Dilthey did, that their place in a sequence may give them special importance. A man's headache may not be very significant by itself but may become so if it occurs during an important meeting or interview. Apart from their temporal relations experiences are also frequently linked by a common theme. Dilthey himself gave such illustrations as repeated visits to an art gallery or the reading of the same book on different occasions. Sometimes it is possible to refer to a sequence of separate but thematically linked experiences as one experience. Seeing Wagner's *Ring* by going to the theatre on several successive evenings is a case in point. If a sequence of experiences is cumulative, as is often the case, this adds another dimension to the meaning. A man's second or third visit to see the same pictures in an art gallery are not like his first visit because of his memories and anticipations.

Dilthey also observed that new experiences shed a different light on old ones so that a man's sense of what his life means to him is constantly changing. He moves into the country and childhood experiences of country life, long dormant in his memory, become relevant. As he perhaps changes from being a business man to a farmer different episodes of his life stand out in his mind as formative. Our earlier metaphor of the string of beads is after all inadequate to convey this sense of flux.

Dilthey not only diagnosed these features in the lives of individuals and used them in his biographical work, he also attributed analogous characteristics to social life and considered them relevant for history and the systematic study of society. His basis for taking this step was that many experiences are shared by numerous individuals either because they are due to events—like floods or earthquakes—which have a widespread effect or because they are produced by common historical, social or cultural factors. The experience of war, inflation or regular seaside holidays can thus be part of the life of a whole country or generation and colour the meaning people give it. The pleasures of sunbathing on crowded beaches may be much sought after in one civilization and unknown in another; the meaning such experiences as holidaying, falling in love or growing up have in different civilizations gives them their distinctive quality.

In the previous chapter we have already noted, from a slightly different angle, the importance of literature for the understanding of the human world. We can now restate Dilthey's view on this matter in terms of meaning. Literature spells out the meaning experiences have for us, making us more conscious of their qualities, and strengthening and perpetuating our responses to them. It even gives quite new meaning to our experiences. So, the literary critic can, by focussing attention on the way experiences are presented in literature, provide valuable material for psychologists, sociologists and social historians.

The experiences of groups, societies and, ultimately, mankind are strung together in a temporal sequence like the individual's and can be related to each other in similar ways. Dilthey, therefore, considered how far we can attribute meaning to history as we do to the lives of individuals. He started by making it very clear where the limits of such an approach lay, for nations and civilizations, unlike people, do not have a relatively fixed life span. There is, usually, no identifiable birthday for a civilization and nothing which makes its end inevitable. He concluded that this makes most talk about the youth or age of a civilization, and any implications drawn from it, vague and misleading. The other obvious, but crucial, difference between individuals and groups, which Dilthey stressed, is that nations or civilizations do not have minds, wills or memories. A man's consciousness, his recollections of the past and anticipations of the future give meaning and unity to his life. If the lives of whole groups of people are to have such a meaning and unity it can only be provided by communication between individuals.

It was Dilthey's conviction that only individual human beings think, feel and pursue purposes. Meaning can, therefore, strictly speaking only arise in individuals because, as we have already seen, it arises from the contact of a consciousness with its environment. History, if it is to be meaningful, must ultimately be about individual human beings. As he put it himself, 'The whole fabric of the historical-social world to which the human studies refer, consists of persons whose experiences can be experienced or understood' (Vol. VII, p.312).[6] Because he was a resolute empiricist and anti-metaphysician he rejected any idea that such concepts as 'nation', 'age' or 'state' are entities which, like human beings, possess consciousness, spirit, will, feelings or a memory. So, to avoid absurdity, such phrases as 'the spirit of an age', 'the popular will', 'a nation's ambitions', 'collective feeling' or 'a folksoul' can only be used metaphorically.

In this Dilthey was entirely at one with the more recent view known as methodological individualism.[7] Unlike some of its adherents, however, he thought it was not only useful but essential for the study of social-historical reality to refer to collective entities, provided one did not mistake them for super-individuals. Groups of people can share ideas, feelings and experiences, have common aims and arrive at collective decisions by communication with each other. Because during the last war a lot of English people experienced the German raids and remained undismayed, talked about them and read about them in the papers, we can speak of England's experience of the raids and response to them. Where individuals have agreed and joined in common action we can talk about a family decision, a cabinet plan or a national policy. In this sense, and in this sense alone, collectives, like nations or civilizations, have experiences, think or act.

Indeed, Dilthey's empiricist approach, solidly based as it is on the examination of expressions, takes the argument a step further. The cabinet decision is there in front of us in a cabinet paper. What the individual members of the cabinet thought and argued may well remain a matter of speculation and hypothesis. So in this, as in very many cases, we are compelled to start from a collective view or decision. All that is necessary to be scientific is that we know what we are doing and remember that by talking about such things as the spirit of an age or the purposes of a nation we are not providing explanations of the affinities between various social and cultural phenomena but merely descriptions of facts which can only be explained by empirical investigation.

Once we have explained the sense in which collective bodies can have experiences we can apply some of the conclusions reached about the experiences of individuals. These acquire their meaning from the elementary experiences of which they are made up and from the wider contexts in which they stand. The second world war, for instance, was a distinctive experience for a generation and consisted of more specific experiences such as air-raids, rationing, the blackout and conscription. It was made more significant because it brought Hitler's rule to an end and increased Russia's power. *When* an experience occurs also gives it significance. The dropping of the first atomic bomb *after* the end of the European war is a case in point.

Experiences are nodal points of meaning in the historical as well as in the individual sphere. How a community actually experiences nature, industrialization or a change of social relationships is the product of many factors of which theoretical awareness may, or may not, be one. But even before they are fully understood and analysed they colour the life of a community. As Dilthey himself put it 'Experiences, though conditioned by social changes and scientific development, emancipate themselves for a time from the chains of conceptual thought and so affect people's minds' (Vol. II, p.437).[8]

Thematically linked experiences acquire particular importance in the social world. They are organised, coordinated and institutionally supported. Dilthey considered that religion, for example, was based on, and revolved around, religious experiences. But these became a social reality in the form of churches, clerical hierarchies, congregations, synods, Sunday services, burial rites and processions which channel, encourage or interpret the religious experiences. Much the same applies to music, art or education. Dilthey called the more or less formally organized and institutionalized coordination of such homogeneous experiences 'cultural systems'. He put it as follows '. . . the cultural systems in which the purposive cooperation of the social, historical world is actively real, consist of experiences and relations between them' (Vol. VII, p.307).[9] Thus meaningful experiences give rise to meaningful social arrangements.

Another sub-class of the human studies, the examination of systems of interactions, is also concerned with the contexts in which experiences stand but, in this case, it is with the interrelationships between different types of experiences. The quality of religious experiences may colour secular things like trade or industry. Industrialization may change the meaning of marriage. Through these links, too, social life as a whole acquires meaning.

So far we have traced the part of Dilthey's theory of non-linguistic meaning which centres on experience. Experiences are meaningful units which combine into meaningful structures and give meaning to the objects experienced. But Dilthey also explored the different lines of approach (including an enquiry into the meaning of actions) necessary to supplement this way of looking at meaning. Actions, we have seen, have meaning as expressions because they reveal the agent's intentions to the observer. Important though this is, it is obviously only part of the story, for it is rarely the sole, and not very often the main, business of actions to communicate something. When I ask what the chancellor's action in raising taxes means, I do not primarily want to know what it tells me about the chancellor's mental life. I am concerned with his purpose and the means chosen to achieve it and expect some such answer as 'It is an effort to control inflation by reducing the borrowing requirements of the government'. If an action had no discernible purpose it would be meaningless and possibly could not even be considered as an action at all. Equally, if the measures chosen had no intelligible bearing on the aim (if the chancellor for example had done nothing but tax pickled gherkins), we would still call them meaningless.

We also talk about the meaning of actions in terms of their *likely* consequences which may be quite different from the consequences aimed at and possibly even in conflict with them. Seen in this light the chancellor's actions may mean dearer cigarettes, perhaps even increased inflation. This type of meaning may only emerge gradually after the event and change as further consequences unfold. This is true of individual as well as corporate actions, everyday ones and acts of historical importance. It should be obvious that Dilthey's clarifications, though not exactly startling by themselves, provide guidelines for practical research and account for the fact that successive generations always rewrite history. Students of sociology will recognize the means–ends pattern of explanation and the contrast between intended and unintended consequences as themes they have encountered in their own subject.

All these together, the value and significance of events, the meaning of experiences and their relationships, the purposes of actions and their consequences, make up the meaning of life and history. It contrasts sharply with linguistic meaning (or, indeed, the meaning of any expression) because neither life, nor the experiences and notions of which it consists, point to something outside themselves. There are, nevertheless, features common to linguistic and non-linguistic meaning which help to justify a common concept. In both spheres meaning is constituted by the relationship between parts and the whole they form. Just as a word contributes to and, in turn, receives meaning from the sentence in which it stands, so individual experiences join to make the meaning of life but have their meaning determined by the wider context. Expressions like actions have a purpose, and means–ends relationships constitute meaning in both spheres. Both expressions and actions tend to make an impact—they may, for instance, cheer or intimidate us, and this too contributes to their meaning.

Even more important than these parallel features are the links between them. One of these is that expressions, and the use of language in particular, are an important and pervasive part of life. We constantly and in numerous ways express ourselves; our actions and bodily movements, and the changes we produce in the world around us, are the outer manifestations of an inner mental reality which contributes immeasurably to the meaning life has for us. Indeed, if we were not capable of forming concepts in language we would not be able to evaluate objects and events, form purposes, make fine distinctions within reality and thus classify things on a more than elementary level. So whatever meaning life has for us is seen through the prism of language. This is another reason why Dilthey attributed such importance to the poet whose experiences he says are 'significant' (*Experience and Poetry*, p.118), insisting 'What is experienced is raised to universal meaning in poetry' (Vol. VII, p.207).[10] Clearly the poet's speciality is his concern for refining and perfecting the verbal communication of meaning.

Because verbal meaning colours and makes accessible the meaning we perceive in life, understanding—defined as the grasping of meaning—can pass smoothly from meaning in one sense to meaning in the other. Understanding another person involves, in the first resort, understanding his words or gestures. It also means grasping the content of what he is communicating, that is, his point of view, the way he sees and experiences things. Students of the human world cannot, without detriment to their subject, ignore the fact that the individuals and groups they study have already interpreted their own nature, their doings and the situations they find themselves in. These interpretations are at least as important as any facts, because people can only act on what they believe to be true or important. (Not the fact that someone has an infectious illness, but my belief that he has—even if mistaken—will keep me away. Not the fact that I can do him good, but my belief that it is my duty to try, will bring me to his bedside.) So a good deal of what the social scientist has to do is to interpret interpretations. It is, therefore, important that what we understand as we take in the meaning of a person's words is the meaning he attributes to particular experiences, to his actions, or even to his life as a whole. It is in this sense that understanding becomes the comprehension of both linguistic and non-linguistic meaning.

In addition to these various parallels, affinities and relations between meanings which refer to something and those which do not, Dilthey stressed that one makes the other possible. Ultimately he provided a general philosophic framework for a theory of language by tracing its roots in life. We can only use language meaningfully because life is meaningful to us. We can recognize words as physical manifestations of something mental *because* we ourselves are compounded of body and mind. (If I am aware of my teeth chattering in fear this is part of a meaningful experience before it becomes a sign to be understood.) We can use language purposefully and recognize it as such *because* the pursuit of ends is part of the meaning of our lives. Language can be given complex structures *because* the mind has a structure of its own which structures its experience. (In other words we know from our inner experience how parts fit into a whole.) The forming of general concepts on which language depends would be impossible if the qualities of objects or events did not stand out in our experience as important or interesting and, therefore, meaningful.

Even the fact that expressions refer to something beyond themselves, though it has no parallel in the meaning of experiences or life, has its roots in that meaning. Dilthey suggested, though he did not elaborate it into a thesis, that the origin of our capacity for using expressions lies in the distinction which reflective consciousness makes between its own ideas and the objects of which they are ideas. (This is not a distinction which coincides with mind and body, or inner and outer. The object to which my idea refers may, for instance, be a previous state of mind.) This was referred to in his biography of Schleiermacher (p.264) where he said Humboldt had proved 'that the reflective activity of the I cannot rest content with contrasting the representation and the represented purely and ideally but strives to perceive outside itself the idea visibly shaped in language'.

So, at the very root of language, lies man's remarkable capacity for detaching the image from the thing and, therefore, for thinking about it when it is not present. This is what enables us to recall the past, anticipate the future, and envisage what is distant in space. Even the higher animals cannot detach images from objects—or can only do so in a most elementary form. Therefore, unlike man, they are compelled to live in the here and now. This is why only man has been able to develop proper languages and, with their help, culture, morality and history. Indeed—and this is the point of Humboldt's remark, quoted with obvious approval by Dilthey—by this unique capacity we are not only enabled, but stimulated, to develop language.

We have seen, then, that the different senses of meaning are related to each other in several ways. For the sake of clarity it is necessary to distinguish them more sharply than Dilthey usually did. But it is equally necessary to defend the retention of the single term because it points to the fact that the various issues raised are closely interwoven. Above all, Dilthey linked the subject-matter of the human studies—the non-linguistic meanings of life—to their methodology (which concerns the study of meaningful expressions).

Dilthey's theory of meaning forms one of the corner stones of his whole philosophy. His theories of understanding and of expressions are the others. Together they form the basis on which his epistemology of the human studies rests.

9

The Critique of Historical Reason

The idea of a critique of historical reason, first conceived in his youth, was to occupy Dilthey until the end of his life. When he gave this title to his most ambitious philosophical work (the fragments of which are reproduced in Vol. VII) he wanted to stress his profound and lasting interest in history as well as his desire to justify his practice as a historian of ideas and the views of the so-called historical school, represented by men like Ranke and Niebuhr, to whom he felt indebted. What, he asked, is involved in historical research which enables the historian to tell a meaningful and reliable story? How can he grasp and convey adequately the changing pattern of events in terms of general concepts and bridge the gulf which divides generation from generation, age from age, and, indeed, individual from individual? Though specifically about history these questions have a wider application because man is a historical being whose cultural aspirations and social relations all have historical aspects and the answers throw light on the whole field of the human studies.

Dilthey posed these questions not only in his *Critique of Historical Reason* but in many other works and tried to answer them on different levels. He was interested in the specific methods of acquiring historical knowledge such as the use of archives, letters and autobiographies, the emendation of texts by philology and many other topics of interest to specialists. (The general methodology he developed will be discussed in the next chapter.) But the more fundamental, epistemological, issues lying behind

123

these questions, also emerged gradually in his many discussions of meaning, understanding and experiences. In his *Critique of Historical Reason* Dilthey intended to face these issues squarely because by 'reason' he meant our basic capacity for knowledge and, therefore, by 'historical reason' our capacity to know the historical and, indeed, the human world in general. So this incomplete work sketches his theory of knowledge of the human studies. We have reached the philosophic core of his thinking and must follow some of his philosophic arguments.

By using the term critique Dilthey defined, from the outset, his own epistemological approach to the questions he had posed. He was consciously and deliberately following Kant who had called his three main works 'critiques', so it will help to look briefly at what Kant meant by a critique and how he envisaged its functions.

The subject-matter of each of Kant's three critiques is a capacity of the human mind. *The Critique of Pure Reason* deals with our power to know the world, *The Critique of Practical Reason* with the power of reason to guide our actions, and *The Critique of Judgment* with our ability to make aesthetic and teleological judgments. In each case, Kant took it for granted that this capacity actually existed. So the first *Critique*—which served as Dilthey's main epistemological model—starts from the assumption that we do know the world around us. Kant did not think it was the philosopher's job to doubt what common sense accepted, and then allay the doubt; this, he argued, only brought discredit to philosophy by appearing to set up Aunt Sallies in order to knock them down with contrived arguments. The problem is not *if* we can know the world around us, do mathematical calculations or arrive at moral principles, but *how* we are able to do it. So Kant defines epistemology in the first *Critique* as the study of what is involved in, or presupposed by, our cognitive achievements.

Non-philosophers may wonder what the problem which makes such philosophic probing necessary, really is. We have no doubt that ordinary observation as well as science can give us knowledge and that whatever errors or inaccuracies may creep in, they can usually be corrected by further observation or scientific work. Clearly, we do not need philosophy to acquire knowledge, for men observed the world before the dawn of philosophy and Newton produced his theories before Kant had put pen to paper. To understand what prompts philosophers like Kant, who himself made these points, to persist with their inquiries, it may be helpful to follow his arguments a few steps further.

Though Kant agreed with the common-sense view that seeing a cow (let us say) gives us genuine knowledge, he did not accept that this process of cognition was something simple which required no further explanation; nor could he accept the kind of explanation we are likely to give—if pressed: we know there is a cow because we can see it and we can see it because it is there to transmit its image. Kant did not think that such answers accounted for the confidence with which we consider such knowledge reliable and reject such possibilities as that the cow could suddenly vanish into thin air. (We shall see that Dilthey referred to this point and talked about 'the validity and necessity of knowledge'.) To explain these characteristics Kant proposed the philosophic hypothesis that they were due to the active part the human mind played in the process of cognition. If this were not so, if knowledge was just a matter of passively receiving an image projected by some outer reality, there would be no reason for considering our knowledge reliable and expecting things to happen in necessary and, therefore, predictable ways. Reality could be capricious or follow laws too complicated for us to grasp. To believe that cows do not suddenly vanish into thin air because they never have done so in our experience, is only a habit of thought not a reason. But if we can show that the human mind always functions in the same way, by imposing its own patterns on the impressions it receives, then the world as we know it will inevitably possess these patterns.

This point can best be illustrated by a frequently used analogy; if green spectacles were irremovably fixed in front of our eyes we should see everything tinged with green; we might not know what the next moment would show us but we should be certain that, whatever it was, it would, necessarily, be green. We can reverse the argument to make the analogy to Kant's reasoning even closer. If everything we saw were green and so we expected it to go on being green it would be natural for us to assume that reality was green. But to Kant this was a very audacious and questionable assumption. Why should we be able to rely on reality continuing to be green or unobserved parts of it being as green as those we have seen? It is much more reasonable to assume that the observer is conditioned to see everything green and this will also allow us to anticipate the greenness of future experiences with absolute confidence.

We must remember that this is only an analogy and has its limitations. Kant is not talking about colours because his argument only holds if he can show that the characteristics of the mind imposed on experience are themselves necessary ingredients of the cognitive processes; if this were not so, as is the case with seeing green, then it may be due to a temporary state (jaundice or wearing glasses which one can take off) and knowledge remains uncertain.

What the mind, according to Kant, must supply is the unity and order which the senses, by themselves, cannot provide; it does so by its own spontaneous and autonomous activity which is, therefore, presupposed in our experience. So what we know about the world through reference to this activity *precedes* experience (i.e. is *a priori* in Kant's terminology).

For the purpose of understanding Dilthey's epistemology we need take only one more step into Kant's philosophy. He thought he could formulate the rules or principles according to which the mind organizes empirical material by analysing the forms taken by our judgments about the world. He called the principles he arrived at by this analysis the categories, listing twelve, of which those of substance and causality are the most important. To explain more fully what he meant by a category and how he arrived at it, it is best to give an illustration in terms of one of them. Our judgments frequently attribute a cause to some event—that electricity in the air causes a thunderstorm or that a burst cylinder caused the car to stop. These judgments presuppose the categorical principle that everything must have a cause. That we believe this is evident from the fact that we would consider a man not wrong but absurd if, because he could not find a fault in our car, he suggested that there was no cause for the breakdown. But this principle cannot be derived from experience for we can never claim to have experienced everything and there is no logical reason for concluding that a particular event had a cause because we had always found other events had causes.

Though this is only a sketch of what has often been described as the greatest revolution in philosophic thought it should help to make clear what Dilthey wanted to convey when he called his work a critique and adapted the concept of categories to his own purpose. He was undoubtedly influenced by, and accepted, a good many of Kant's general assumptions, his style of argument and conclusions. He criticized some points and, above all, considered Kant's work incomplete, proposing as one of his main tasks to supplement his achievement. Kant had revealed the foundations on which our knowledge of the physical world rested; it was up to him, Dilthey, to do the same for our knowledge of man. The aim of his own critique was to lay bare the presuppositions on which understanding the cognitive process, crucial to the human studies, is based. (Those who have read, or are likely to read, Kant in an English translation should be warned that, though the term understanding figures prominently there it means roughly the use of reason in empirical contexts.) True to Kant's approach, Dilthey did not doubt, and did not think he needed to prove, that historical knowledge, comprehension of literary works or insight into the mental life of our fellowmen was possible. His critique was to reveal the fundamental conditions on which these achievements rest.

In pursuing his epistemological investigation Dilthey, like other philosophers including Kant, sought to satisfy his intellectual curiosity. It is as hard to explain the charms of philosophy to the indifferent as it is those of mountaineering to the uninterested. But Dilthey combined more practical aims with his detached curiosity. In the human studies there was more doubt and uncertainty, more bias and controversy, than in the sciences. Firm foundations for the study of man had yet to be laid involving various steps which all engaged Dilthey's attention: a clear and consistent use of concepts which reflected the facts as precisely as possible and a methodology, based on comparisons between successful and unsuccessful research, which could establish guidelines for future investigations. Needed too, was a clear conception of how the different disciplines were related to each other and could cooperate. In his opinion the only proper framework for these various undertakings was a critique which penetrated to the epistemological foundations of understanding and examined its powers and limitations.

The main reason why we have to go back to philosophic fundamentals if we are to get our research right is because it is inevitably governed by general presuppositions. If they have been accepted thoughtlessly or as a result of faulty arguments, they may be confused, inadequate and even contradictory, obscuring issues by over-emphasizing one factor and ignoring others. Because very broad general considerations persuaded medieval scholars to place excessive stress on the authority of the written word philosophic arguments were needed to persuade their successors of the sixteenth and seventeenth centuries to give more attention to observation and experiment. In the nineteenth century it was important to argue philosophically that the examination of communications was at least as important a source of infor- mation in the human studies as observations of behaviour. To put it crudely, good philosophy is necessary because what we do is often governed by bad philosophy.

Dilthey shared Kant's most important epistemological conclu- sions, saying:

He discovered the epistemological procedure which seeks the conditions that make valid and necessary knowledge possible in the thinking subject; he found the most general of these conditions to be the synthesizing power which links the multiplicity of what is given into systematic unity. He proved incontrovertibly that experience and the empirical sciences are only possible through the synthesizing power of thought and that—on the other hand—this thought can only achieve knowledge within the realm of what can be experienced. (Vol. IV, p.44)'[1]

He also agreed with Kant that 'the *a priori* in us is our autonomous activity' (Vol. IV p.536)[2] but he diverged from him in his conception of the nature of our presuppositions and of the way we know about them. For Kant the *a priori* presuppositions were timeless, formal, principles corresponding to the laws of logic; to Dilthey they were the changing assumptions which people developed, used and discarded in the course of history. 'Kant's *a priori*', he wrote, 'is dead because the presuppositions which, as I understand it, really condition our consciousness are parts of a living historical process, develop and have their own history . . . the vital processes of history affect even the apparently rigid and dead conditions of our thinking' (*Nachlass*, N33, Vol. II, p.119). He argued[3] that even our most fundamental concepts and such basic rules as those of logic are historical products with a development which we can trace empirically. 'History is the indispensible preliminary to systematic philosophy because concrete consciousness of the self, which can be analysed but not separated from knowledge, is historical' (Vol. VIII, p.191).

Dilthey could see that a circle was involved in the attempt to discover the presuppositions of empirical knowledge by empirical investigation because the same cognitive process is both examined and used for the examination. But he thought that this was inevitable and did not vitiate the procedure, a view fundamental to his whole epistemology which must be looked at more closely. Dilthey thought that our cognitive procedures were inevitably circular because there was no firm, philosophic, starting point. He thought the search for it ill conceived and that the whole tradition of modern philosophy had been led astray by Descartes' attempt to erect a theory of knowledge on the basis of something which could not be doubted. In practice we can be certain of many things, prominent among them the findings of careful introspection and the results of painstaking science, but closer inspection shows that our assurance depends on outside factors. Obtaining knowledge is like walking through a morass. We can pull one leg out of the mud by resting on the other and when that begins to sink we must shift our weight once more. Everything can be examined critically, and that is the aim of philosophy but, even as we submit one belief to criticism, we must take others for granted. To assure itself of its knowledge the mind commits itself to a constant to and fro movement which occurs on all levels of cognition. 'Philosophy', Dilthey wrote to York (July 1896, p.220), 'has no universally valid starting point free from all presuppositions. The starting point is subject to a circle. We can only diagnose facts as incontrovertible (which is, after all, at issue) by thinking, analysing and, therefore, judging and inferring. Hence the validity of thought processes for ascertaining facts is presupposed.' This circle occurs even in the simple case of recognizing objects. For us to know what a polar bear is like someone must have seen one, but how could he ever know that he had seen a polar bear unless he knew what they were like? An analogous problem occurs in what Dilthey called the hermeneutic circle. We cannot pinpoint the precise meaning of a word unless we read it in its context, i.e. the sentence or paragraph in which it occurs. But how can we know what the sentence means unless we have first understood the individual words? Logically there is no escape from this absence of priority; in practice we solve the problem by a kind of mental shuttlecock movement.

Dilthey drew two specific conclusions about epistemology from the circularity of all knowledge. First, we cannot step outside or beyond our experience. Among his various formulations of this point is the insistence which we have already encountered that we cannot go behind life. Confined as man is to the human point of view, he can only disentangle from within the total situation in which he finds himself. When the philosopher starts on his analysis he is already familiar with the world around him and has learned to employ the presuppositions he now wants to examine. So, and this is Dilthey's second conclusion, the situations we have to account for are invariably complex and already structured so there can be no certain knowledge which, being independent of anything else, can provide the foundations of all knowledge.

There is no logically compelling reason for choosing a single insight or principle for one's starting point, but what we can do is balance two or three against each other. Introspective awareness of our own mental processes is basic and indispensible if we want to understand people and cultural products; but how could we understand ourselves if we had not learned a language and, through it, how to make conceptual distinctions? We must be able to compare ourselves with others and learn from literature the potentialities of love or jealousy. One road leads from my mind to that of others, a second from knowledge of others back to self-knowledge.

There are also ways of looking at the fundamental processes of cognition which supplement each other. On the one hand, they are the source of—and therefore the starting point for—all knowledge; on the other, like all mental processes, they can become the subject of inquiry. If we treat them as the sources, we are adopting an epistemological point of view; if as the subject of inquiry, a psychological one. This is why Dilthey argued that epistemology and psychology were interdependent.[4] The former provides the basis for all knowledge, including psychological knowledge, while the latter accounts for all mental processes including those of cognition.

Dilthey undertook the epistemological analysis of understanding in order to supplement the list of cognitive processes already analysed by Kant but he also envisaged that, by doing so, he could revolutionize epistemology as a whole. To know almost anything involves the cooperation of different cognitive processes. (Just as understanding a sentence involves hearing or seeing it first, so knowing about the planetary motions requires understanding concepts and theories.) This is why emphasizing and analysing one of these cognitive processes changes the whole picture.

The epistemological question which Dilthey posed was 'what makes it possible for us to understand human beings and their creation?' (or 'what is presupposed in such an understanding?'). To answer this question he formulated two very general principles and explained how they worked by referring to a number of categories. His first principle is succinctly and vividly expressed in his assertion that 'understanding is the rediscovery of the I in the Thou' (Vol. VII, p.189). On the surface this asserts something obvious, familiar and non-controversial. I understand what someone means when he says, 'I am sad', because I attribute to him what I would be feeling if I had said it. The same applies to understanding something which does not involve words. I understand why someone makes such an effort at tennis because I know what it is like to want to win at a game. Understanding succeeds by supplementing what we observe with our senses, with our own inner experiences. 'We understand human life, history and all the hidden depths of the human mind because we experience these transitions and effects and so become aware of the structure which embraces all passions, sufferings and human destinies (Vol. V, p.206).[5]

Underlying this obvious point is an important and not easily defined assumption that there is a common human nature or, to put it more cautiously, that men share fundamental features. The emphasis here is not on *all* men sharing significant characteristics in the sense in which any discipline must assume that it is dealing with a uniform subject-matter (chemistry, for example, assuming that all gases have common properties) but in the really significant requirement that *observer* and *observed* should share common features. But how extensive is this requirement? If we were all alike any effort at understanding would be superfluous for it would be automatic; without effort we would recognize ourselves in others. But, obviously, we are not that much alike; there are considerable differences between individuals and these are greater between people of different ages or civilizations. How far do these differences prevent or inhibit understanding? Can white men understand black men, middle-class intellectuals workers, men women, heterosexuals homosexuals or modern historians ancient warriors? Far from being abstractly philosophical, these questions are very serious and urgently require answers today. It is of critical importance to decide *what* must be assumed as common if understanding is to be possible. As we shall see, Dilthey tried to clarify this issue both in his theory of categories and in his projected anthropology.

Dilthey's second epistemological principle is that the mind can understand what the mind has created. He probably owed this principle to the Italian thinker, Vico, whom he occasionally mentions and who first formulated this idea in the eighteenth century.[6] This principle covers the whole sphere of the objectifications of mind from words and gestures to institutions, laws, religions, the processes of history and the working of society. Thus, the two principles supplement each other by dealing with different aspects of understanding. We have seen in Chapter 6 that understanding people is different from understanding their expressions and that these different forms of understanding are interdependent. We could not understand the creations of human minds unless we understood the minds, but understanding the creations is necessary if we are to bridge the gap between us and people very different from us. (The modern historian, for instance, can only understand the men of the Renaissance by reading their literature and looking at their art.)

In his attempt to explain more fully how we can understand

man and his creations Dilthey followed further along Kant's path. He greatly appreciated Kant's achievement in demonstrating that categories are involved in our knowledge of the physical world. He thought it was Kant's 'great discovery' that 'metaphysical presuppositions, namely the categories, underlie the forms our judgments take' (Vol. VI, p.44).[7] What was now needed, he thought, was to extend this list of categories by adding those specially involved in understanding the human world; he called them 'the categories of life'. Because his ideas on the subject were largely developed in the last years of his life they remain incomplete; they are, nevertheless, his most profoundly stimulating contribution to the epistemology of the human studies.

Dilthey's main categories of life are inner–outer, means–ends (or purpose), value, part–whole, power, meaning and temporality. He did not consider this list complete; as categories are historical products new ones emerge (development, he thought, was an example of a relatively recent one) and the list can never be completed. Nor was he willing to commit himself to a definite order of priority among the categories though, at times, he picked out one or the other as particularly important or as taking pride of place. He wrote, for instance, 'Temporality is contained in life as its first categorical characterization which is fundamental to all the others' (Vol. VII, p.192),[8] but he could have said—and in some cases did say—the same about other categories. This lack of a consistent arrangement is, no doubt, partly due to the fact that he was not able to finish his work on the categories, but it also reflects his view that they, like so much in the world, were interdependent. There is, in consequence, no particular significance in the order in which we shall deal with them.

When we discussed expressions and their meaning we noted that they are physical objects or events conveying an idea which itself reflects the fact that behind man's physical behaviour lie mental processes. Dilthey considered this a general presupposition for any study of man, a category which he called 'inner and outer'. It is a presupposition because we cannot conceive of coming across expressions by chance or by the sort of systematic search we use to find a rare animal. Unless we assume that man has an inner life which is conveyed by physical manifestations we could never recognise an expression and, therefore, never communicate. Just as Kant's category of cause stipulates that we must always look for a cause, so Dilthey's principle requires us to look for an inner side (meaning or reference) of a range of outer manifestations. (In both cases we are talking about the form judgments take, namely attributing causes in one case, meaning in the other, while any specific cause or meaning can only be supplied by empirical investigation.)

The category of purpose (or means and ends as he sometimes called it) is another fundamental presupposition about human life which we have already come across. That human beings act purposefully and that what they do must be explained in terms of their choices of means to ends is not something we discover only in particular cases. On the contrary, we could not recognize a greeting, a warning or a skilled operation unless we assumed that there was an intention behind the sounds or gestures. Only then can we consider *what* the purpose or intention is and how well the means are adjusted to the ends. No student of the social sciences needs to be told how important these considerations are.

The presence of value, i.e. the fact that human beings make value judgments in terms of their likes and dislikes and their assessments of the consequences of events or actions, gives rise to another category, for we cannot analyse human life without reference to values.

The category of part and whole represents the assumption that the entities with which the human studies have to deal (i.e. people, families, nations, documents, legal codes or literary works) consist of parts and are parts of larger wholes and that this is an important factor in explaining them. The principle that we must analyse men and their creations in these terms is of obvious methodological importance and we shall return to it in the next chapter.

Particularly interesting is the category of power which is what Dilthey called the presupposition that we are in constant dynamic interaction with our environment, affecting it, and being affected by it. What Dilthey had in mind is the kind of force or power we are aware of when, for example, we make an effort to roll away a stone or feel ourselves threatened or intimidated by something. It resembles, or can even be described as a sub-class of, causality but it is something much more personal than being aware of a regular connection between thunder and lightning and attributing it to some hidden force. This is probably why primitive man tended to see causal connections in terms of conscious beings impinging upon each other (the light defeating the darkness, a river god taking his revenge on man). The impersonal category of causality was developed later and, in the case of physical nature, replaced that of power. But in the human world it remains an essential presupposition.

Dilthey called the assumption that things become meaningful by being related to recollections of the past the category of meaning. We could not, for example, recognize a rose (thus giving meaning to our experience of seeing a particular flower) unless we had learned the concept and seen roses in the past. On a more complex level, my encounter with a particular person is given its meaning by the fact that I have known him for twenty years. Unless we could presuppose this relationship to the past even our knowledge of the physical world, let alone that of the human world, would be impossible.

There is, however, an ambiguity in Dilthey's account of the category of meaning. Because meaning plays an important part in his philosophy, all the categories can be described as different ways in which meaning is constituted and recognized. For instance, when we specify the purpose of an action or the value of an experience, we are describing its meaning. In this sense all the categories are categories of meaning and this must not be confused with *the* category of meaning in its more specific sense.

The category of temporality is, probably, the most intriguing of all and the one most directly linked to Dilthey's project of a critique of historical reason. His highly original treatment of temporality has had particular influence—for example on existentialism—and I have left its discussion until last because it requires fuller treatment. We encountered something of Dilthey's analysis of temporality when we considered his conception of how the flow of life, in which experiences are linked, contributes to the meaning we give to our existence. Our experience of time is awareness of a flow in which the anticipated future becomes the real present which, in turn, becomes the past that exists only in our memories and the traces it leaves behind. Even moments of experience have this temporal structure. I could never 'hear' a sentence unless I remembered the first word as I heard the second and anticipated more to follow. The interlocking of the three temporal dimensions, future, present and past, is the condition for all knowledge because only in the present do we have experiences which put us in touch with reality, only the past provides us with memories which give meaning to them, and only the future can bring confirmation of our anticipations. This conception of time as a continuous succession of moments which have duration and a temporal structure is time as we actually experience it; according to its content and our moods it sometimes passes slowly and sometimes quickly. Dilthey contrasted this with the conception of clocktime as used in the sciences, which is a uniform succession of equal and empty moments.

By talking of man's temporality Dilthey wanted to stress that the way we experience time is, and must be, presupposed in all our judgments about man. In these temporal dimensions are not only a condition of knowledge but a characteristic of the subject-matter. Human beings are affected by their recollections of the past and anticipations of the future as well as by the actual circumstances of the present, while everything else is only affected by such circumstances and (with the exception of higher animals which do so to a very limited degree) neither remembers nor looks ahead. This makes man a historical being. 'The structure of mental life contains within itself the schema—the scaffolding as it were—of all the historical processes which originate from the interaction of poeple' (Vol. IV, p.559).[9] This applies both to individuals and their lives and to large groups and their history.

It is worth mentioning in conclusion that the category of temporality provides a link for other categories. Dilthey thought that the categories of meaning, value and purpose were related to each other because each was concerned with one of the temporal dimensions, meaning with the past, value with the present, and purpose with the future. This is only one of the suggestions which Dilthey made about the interrelations between the categories. It is one of the aspects of his theory of categories which he did not elaborate fully and consistently.

Kant's theory of knowledge stipulated that the knowing mind, in order to use the categories, must possess unity to impose on its material. Dilthey, in his attempt to see the knowing subject as a being in whose veins real blood flowed, adapted Kant's requirement in his own way. This resulted in a conception of man's mental structure which was ahead of most contemporary psychology. Though Dilthey accepted the traditional view that man's natural mental functions are thinking, feeling and willing (and used this classification in various contexts, for instance, in analysing world-views) he emphasized that they were closely interrelated and indeed all involved in our knowledge of the world. Reality, he had argued at length in an earlier work (*The Origins of our Belief in the Reality of the External World* contained in Vol. V), discloses itself particularly in its resistance to the will, and shows its qualities in the way it affects our feelings. The inter-relationship of these different functions constitutes the structure of the mind and it is this structure as a whole which imparts distinctive qualities to its individual acts. 'By mental structure', he explained, 'I mean the arrangement according to which different types of mental facts are regularly linked in a developed mental life by inner relationships which can be experienced' (Vol. VII, p.15).[10] The natural mental structure consisted, he argued, of such innate links as those between perception, memory, feeling and will. If I see a snarling dog approaching I interpret the situation in the light of my past experience and, as a result, am afraid which, in turn, prompts me to run away. These connections are not logically necessary but part of our basic human nature. We can imagine, Dilthey suggested, a creature who could observe a battlefield, comprehend the situation but feel neither fear nor pity, or who, though feeling fear, did not have the impulse to do something like running away. We happen not to be made like that and our mental processes do not occur in isolation but are interwoven because our thoughts are coloured by our emotions, our perceptions by our judgments and our aspirations by our memories.

Superimposed on this natural mental structure is what Dilthey called the acquired mental structure; it is the product of experience filling in the innate links. The connection between fear and the impulse towards some avoiding action is natural but we must learn to fear speeding motorists and develop the most appropriate response. Civilization creates new objects of fear or desire and culture new ways of responding to them. Fear of the nuclear bomb and the moral and political attitudes produced by it, or addiction to television and its effects on our outlook and behaviour, are developments which have shaped human personality in our own time.

So, how people think and feel, how they perceive the world and what they strive for, is due to a mental structure which has resulted from the moulding influence of physical, social and cultural factors upon the innate configurations of the mind.

It should have become clear that the matters discussed in this chapter—the epistemological principles stipulating a common human nature and the knowability of its products, the categories, and the conception of the mind's structure—can be looked at from two sides. Seen from one side—the side which we have on the whole stressed so far—they are presuppositions of our knowledge of the human world. In other words it could be shown by analysis that they are conditions which must be fulfilled if we are to understand man. They can be spelled out as very general, formal, judgments which imply principles or injunctions. (For instance, the category of temporality can be expressed as 'man is a historical creature' from which the principle that knowledge of man requires a historical approach follows.) As we are confident that we know the human world we can reasonably conclude that these conditions *are* fulfilled, these assertions tenable. We have then justified our presuppositions by philosophic argument.

But, quite obviously, we are already talking about human nature when we refer to the mind's structure or capacities. What, from one side, appears as a presupposition of knowledge is, from the other, part of that knowledge, something we have learned from psychology or history. According to Dilthey there can be no sharp, logical distinction between what we want to know about man and what we must already know to start on our inquiries. Theoretically, we can distinguish between the full knowledge of man which is the goal of empirical research and a broad conception of man which must guide our research but, in practice, the demarcation lines are obscured by their dependence on each other.

Dilthey's conception of the complex relationship between different starting points can be disentangled in terms of his idea of an anthropology which is partly philosophic. Though his references to this topic are extremely sketchy the idea of a philosophic anthropology proved enormously influential and was taken up by the next generation of philosophers, especially Scheler, Heidegger and Plessner whose writings gave wide currency to the concept.

Dilthey qualified his idea that philosophic conceptions of man were possible by insisting on the need for experience, but felt that he had to do more than contrast an empirical with a philosophic anthropology; he had to go back to history as the source of empirical knowledge. 'For history alone', he wrote, 'shows us what man is' (*The Great Poetry of Imagination*, p.34) or, again, 'Man does not discover what he is through speculation about himself or through psychological experiments but through history' (Vol. V, p.181)[11] and 'What man is and what he strives for he only discovers in the development of his nature through the millenia; it is never spelled out in universally valid concepts, only in vital experiences which spring from the depths of his whole being' (Vol. VI, p.37).[12]

On the basis of this historical material an anthropology becomes possible. By this concept Dilthey meant a fairly broadly based, descriptive, analytical and cautiously systematic study of man which overlapped with his conception of a descriptive psychology as he described it in his *Ideas about a Descriptive and Analytical Psychology* (1894). So, in following his use of this term, we must avoid any association with such specialized disciplines as physical or social anthropology. His own description of anthropology and its method is as follows:

Mental life can be illuminated and analysed by different methods. In each of them experience and understanding intertwine, for only understanding encompasses the whole horizon of mental life and only experience illuminates its depths and makes them accessible to understanding. Nearest to life itself is the method which describes and analyses the sequence and coexistence of concrete, mental, states ... this is anthropological method.
Anthropological research is akin to poetry. An experience is imaginatively elaborated according to its inherent meaning and thus the rela-

tionship of the mental process to the surrounding life is concretely described. (Vol. VI, p.305)[13]

It is hardly necessary to add that, though anthropology is based on historical material, it in turn provides the knowledge of human nature without which the historian cannot operate.

Now that we have a general picture of Dilthey's empirical anthropology and its relation to history we can return to the role of a philosophic anthropology within this context. Which, among all the features of human nature which experience reveals, are philosophically significant? The answer is that they are basically the features which have one or the other of the following characteristics. One we have already discussed: if a feature is involved in the cognitive process it is philosophically important as part of the presuppositional framework of the human studies. The other characteristic which makes an aspect of human nature philosophically noteworthy is that it contributes to a picture of man, providing guidelines and criteria for research. Dilthey put this point as follows: 'All the human studies presuppose a type of human nature which serves as a touchstone for their conclusions. This type is something different and something more than that so far developed by psychology. I call its theoretical development anthropology' (*Nachlass*, Vol. C34, II, p.156). To illustrate: if a historical account or the record of a psychological experiment claimed that there was a human being whose emotions never aroused him to any desire for action (say thirst not making him want to drink) we would remain extremely sceptical unless it could be explained by some special cause, such as a disease. In many cases the aspects of human nature which serve as touchstones in this way are the same as those *presupposed* in the process of cognition. Any theory of human nature, for instance, which does not allow for successful understanding between people can be dismissed as absurd because the author must be presumed to want us to understand what *he* is saying. So philosophic anthropology is both the epistemological basis for, and the critical examination of, the human studies.

A discussion of some further aspects of human nature considered crucial by Dilthey has been left for the next chapter because they are directly relevant to his methodology. But, before we turn to this part of Dilthey's philosophy, one more implication of his epistemological approach must be brought out—the relativity of all knowledge.

Dilthey's assumption that the mind superimposes something of its own on sense-impressions is bound to lead to a form of relativity, but one which is innocuous in practice. As long as our common human nature makes us all experience in the same way (as if we all had green spectacles, in our earlier illustration) our knowledge will be relative to the knowing mind, i.e. subjective, but it will also be objective, in the sense of being something on which we could all agree. But if, as Dilthey said, our cognitive powers and the concepts and forms of judgments we use develop in history, and may even vary according to background or temperament, then no basis for agreement remains. The question arises, can there be any knowledge which is universally valid? 'The way knowledge is combined at a particular time', Dilthey said, 'is conditioned by the state of consciousness and is always its subjective and transitory expression; ideals of life and world-views are always based on frames of mind and are, therefore, only valid for the historical period of their dominance' (Vol. VIII, p.7).[14] As a supporter of the historical school Dilthey accepted the historical relativity of all knowledge and, as a historian of ideas, was interested in the way in which man's basic concepts and presuppositions changed and affected his outlook. Indeed Dilthey hailed this historical approach as a liberating force which undermined dogmatism. Yet he was fully, and indeed painfully, aware that this relativism, if accepted without qualifications, led straight into the abyss of complete scepticism. If all views are relative, in the sense of being seriously coloured by their particular origin, the whole concept of truth is undermined. No certainties remain in either science or philosophy and no authority behind moral judgments. Deprived of firm foundations political choice becomes feeble and arbitrary.

Dilthey sought an escape from this dilemma by putting his own demarcation line—fluid though it is—between what is due to a common human nature and what to historical forces. 'The same analysis which makes the past of human thought its object reveals the relativity of every system but, at the same time, it makes these systems comprehensible in terms of human nature and the nature of objects; it explores the laws of their formation, their common structure, their main forms and the inner structure and principle of formation of these forms.' (Vol. VIII, p.12).[14] So what is due to a common human nature is, if not free from all relativity, capable of being universally valid. This does not provide a simple guideline, however, because, as Dilthey saw very clearly, our natural endowments are entangled with, and overlaid by, the acquired structure of the mind. We know there are firm foundations but we can never be absolutely sure that we are standing on them. Once more an absolute starting point eludes us and we are left with circular arguments.

Dilthey thought that this reflected the situation scholars actually find themselves in. While retaining the ideal of objective truth they must accept its elusiveness and live with the difficulty of disentangling the core of truth from the temporal guise imposed by the fact that the human nature on which they rely is itself historically moulded.

But Dilthey stressed that we gain a *measure* of objective truth when we recognize that something is true within its historical limitations. We may have to concede, for instance, that certain geometrical statements about spatial relationships only follow if we accept the axioms of a particular geometry which is the product of a particular age. But that the one follows from the other is not relatively but absolutely true. So we can reach a measure of truth even within the changing panorama of historically and conventionally determined views.

Dilthey's epistemology was, as we have seen, focussed on the processes involved in knowing man. But though, as an heir to the Western philosophic tradition, he was profoundly interested in the theory of knowledge for its own sake, he was also concerned with its practical application. This meant that it should provide a basis for a methodology.

10

The methodology of the human studies

'My real goal is a methodology of the human studies', said Dilthey—writing to York in 1884 and describing his work on a sequel to the recently published first volume of the *Introduction to the Human Studies*. He intended to supplement the historical approach of the first volume with a systematic treatment of the human studies which he considered essential (Vol. XIX reproduces his extensive manuscript drafts of this project). But the subject of methodology was not confined to this book; Dilthey raised it in all his work on the human studies from the early drafts for a book on *The Study of the History of the Disciplines concerned with Man, Society and the State* (Vol. XVIII) to *The Critique of Historical Reason* written at the end of his life (Vol. VII) as well as in his historical and aesthetic writings. Though he says much that is original and thought-provoking on this topic he never managed to systematize his ideas to his own satisfaction. If one tries to put them into any kind of order one is apt to minimize their difficulty and lose something of their subtlety and fluidity.

Methodology is more concrete and down to earth than epistemology because it is more directly concerned with the methods of inquiry in different disciplines (but is more abstract and general than the study of particular techniques like spectroscopy or the thematic apperception test). By itself it can no more make people successful investigators than training manuals can transform middle-aged weaklings into Olympic medallists. But it can provide principles for research and criteria for testing its validity by examining—in the light of epistemological principles—successful and unsuccessful investigations. This is how the philosopher can help the progress of the sciences and human studies.

Dilthey's interest in the subject reflected his practical bent for, much as he enjoyed thought and research for their own sake, he was anxious that ideas should be put to practical use. 'The usefulness of methods emerges from their use, just as the test of a knife is if it cuts. Or, putting the same point in another way, Theory follows practice' (Vol. XVIII, p.1). He wanted to establish principles for the study of man because he thought that a proper understanding of man was of paramount importance; he tried to derive these principles from his general epistemological insights and his deductions about the nature of the human world. Different strands of his thought converged therefore in his methodology and can be seen there in relation to each other.

Though specifically interested in the human studies Dilthey did not think that their methodology could be treated in isolation. He envisaged and sketched, but did not elaborate systematically, a whole philosophy of science about the use of different methods in the pursuit of knowledge; this has a strong affinity with the pragmatism of Peirce and Royce. It also anticipated what today is called the 'systems-approach'. This aspect of his work has only been noted recently because it was overshadowed by his methodology of the human studies which was worked out more powerfully and in greater detail. His affinities with the pragmatists, in spite of the very different background and range of interests from which they started, is also noteworthy and makes a close comparative study worthwhile.

Among the reasons which Dilthey gives for treating the human studies in the wider context of a philosophy of science is that any investigation consists of many procedures and mental processes most of which are common to, and indispensable for, all investigations. Observing, logical reasoning, comparing, classifying, abstracting, as well as framing and testing hypotheses or analysing by means of statistical techniques, are used just as much in the human studies as in any science. Even where an intellectual procedure or method is particularly associated with a single discipline—say the evolutionary approach in biology—it may often be fruitfully transferred to other areas. This is why Dilthey believed that the general application of these processes should be examined before their particular applications and combinations with each other in individual disciplines could be traced.

Dilthey's belief that the interdependence of all knowledge implied interdisciplinary cooperation was a further reason why he advocated a close relationship between different human studies as well as between human studies and sciences. Psychologists need physiological data, anthropologists physical measurements, while historians can derive help from carbon dating or the chemical analyses of documents.

But the paramount reason for his refusal to departmentalize disciplines was his empiricism; he emphasized the primacy of full, concrete experience and considered that all the distinctions between such fundamentally different subjects as mind and matter, consciousness and body, were due to the way we pick out features that interest us and so do not necessarily reflect the ultimate nature of things. We have seen already that Dilthey placed great emphasis on the distinction between mind and matter which are the respective subjects of the human studies and the sciences. But he did not consider this a philosophic discovery nor share the preoccupation of traditional metaphysicians with its roots in ultimate reality, because he did not think one could rationally decide whether mind and matter were independent substances or whether one was subordinated to the other, or that it mattered in practice whether mind and matter interacted or ran on parallel courses. The different sides taken on these issues in the history of philosophy had, in his view, no bearing on the growth of the human studies and he considered it sufficient to base himself on the practical, common-sense distinction between matter and mind we make in daily life. I know if I am bored and may, or may not, show it by yawning or fidgeting; a book is a physical object in front of me but it contains ideas. We do not have the slightest difficulty in understanding and accepting these distinctions when we speak of mind, mental content, consciousness and ideas on the one hand, and body, matter and physical objects on the other. To judge the value of these distinctions we must just consider how useful they are for describing, exploring and mastering reality.

Dilthey was determined to start from the rich complexity of experience and base himself on the minimum of theoretical presuppositions for reality, in his own words, 'is what is related to the totality of our consciousness in thought, will and feeling'. Man's perennial effort to know the world is an attempt to catch reality in a conceptual net; as concepts are, inevitably, abstract and general they can never do full justice to the uniqueness and intricacy of individual experiences and the complex ways we respond to them. Dilthey was close enough to the Romantics to echo the idea that 'we murder to dissect'[1] and insisted that this dissection should be tentative and provisional. The distinctions we make are our historically and socially conditioned ways of looking at reality, and so parcelling out the universe in terms of fish and fowl, vegetable and mineral, mind and matter, is convenient and has proved useful but it contains arbitrary and subjective elements and is, at the very least, too neat. The different disciplines like biology, chemistry or sociology are the products of the way we have conceptualized differences within an infinitely complex reality and, therefore, do not deal with separate, self-contained, sections of reality as their respective subjects. Dilthey concluded that we can establish how different disciplines are related to and depend on each other by tracing the way our thinking originally defined their subject-matter.

A simple illustration will show how different disciplines pick out different aspects of the same complex reality. If someone gives a speech (and even identifying this situation involves a measure of selection) various aspects of it can be distinguished and studied. The movements of his speech organs concern the physiologist while the physicist explores the resulting sound-waves; linguists may be interested in the speaker's accent and grammar, psychologists in his attitude, political scientists in what he is saying. Each specialist may go his own way or they may cooperate where there are inter-connections such as those between the speech organs and the sounds produced.

Though Dilthey believed that we divide up reality mentally and parcel it out as subject-matter of the different disciplines according to our convenience he did not think we did this in a completely arbitrary way. He was convinced that our concepts and classifications partly reflect our actual encounters with reality and are corrected by them. The subject-matter, therefore, influences the methods suitable for its investigation and this makes distinctive methods for the human studies necessary. They may overlap with the methods of other disciplines but have features of their own. In the importance he placed on these features, he parted company with J.S. Mill and the positivists. He shared their concern that the human studies should be scientific—in the sense of being systematic, precise and based on well established, empirical, evidence—and retained elements of a sturdy positivism in his work for which he has been attacked by those who adopted and pushed to their limits his suggestions for supplementing the methods of science by others unique to the human disciplines. (Gadamer, for example, thought that Dilthey's positivism was a hangover from early influences to which he had been exposed and had failed to shed as his thought matured.) But he diverged from the full positivist programme which aimed at the ultimate unity of science (including the human disciplines) by extending the use of scientific methods to the latter. Positivists appreciate that there are differences between different disciplines but consider them of secondary importance maintaining that sociology differs no more from chemistry than the latter does from physics. Dilthey tried to demonstrate what an important difference the pervasiveness of mind makes to the study of man.

The term which common sense and common usage suggests for the chief method of the human studies is interpretation. Mind, we have seen, manifests itself in a multiplicity of expressions, some of which are highly complex; though in principle capable of understanding them the mind often encounters difficulties; then the words or gestures, the texts or actions must be interpreted. Unlike understanding, which is a mental process, interpretation can be properly described as a method because it involves a combination of various mental processes some of which are shared with the scientific method. Interpreting a poem or legal clause, like explaining an experimental result, involves reasoning, making comparisons and conjectures, but, unlike its scientific counterpart, it revolves around the process of understanding which is not only its final aim but is involved at every stage of the interpretative process. 'Interpretation' also suggests the main advantages and drawbacks of the human studies: the possibility of entering imaginatively into the subject-matter and the unavoidable element of subjectivity.

Dilthey stressed that interpretation is something which has been practised systematically by human beings from the dawn of history. People always thought it important to interpret their religious traditions and sacred books, their laws and conventions, their myths, legends and epics, because good or bad luck, the fate of the soul after death, life, liberty and the esteem of fellow men in this life depended on getting the answers right. So traditions of interpretation, preserving and developing principles of application and criteria of success as old as man's attempts to explore outer nature, had been established.

The Greeks, because they were extremely interested in the systematic interpretation of their own literature as part of the educational process, had a word for the development of the art of interpretation—hermeneutics. Derived from Hermes (the messenger of the Gods) it came to stand for the methodology—and sometimes for the systematic practice—of interpretation. Dilthey gives us a history of the development of hermeneutics in one of his long essays.[2] After the triumph of Christianity it became an auxiliary discipline of theology because ability to interpret the Bible according to clear and sound principles was very important in the repeated struggles against heretics and the continuous quarrel between different denominations. Dilthey became interested in the subject through his study of Schleiermacher, who was not only a theologian but also a philosopher and interpreter of Plato. He widened the scope of hermeneutics, treating it as the methodology of interpretation of any kind of text and expanding it to include grammatical and stylistic as well as psychological and historical analyses.

Dilthey took Schleiermacher's idea a step further and extended its role so that it became the methodology and key discipline of the human studies. Even in its original—and still primary—application to the interpretation of texts, its relevance to the human studies should be clear because literary works, codes of law, constitutions, letters, business contracts and historical records are important sources of knowledge about human life. But Dilthey extended the scope of hermeneutics further by a number of logical steps. If written words can be systematically interpreted why not spoken words? So the same principles can be applied to speeches, conversations or interview-responses. The next extension follows directly from Dilthey's theory of expressions: if facial expressions, gestures and actions can be meaningful in much the same way as words they can be subjected to the same hermeneutic approach.

Taken one by one these steps are innocuous enough but taken together they amount to a claim that the human world must be studied in a distinctive way because it is permeated by expressions of mind. The need to interpret these expressions makes the hermeneutic approach paramount. Dilthey's crucial argument can be put in terms of a thesis which considerably influenced subsequent philosophers and theoreticians of the human studies and may yet stimulate contemporary thought still further. Far-reaching though its implications are, it can be put quite simply: a good deal of what practitioners of the human studies have to do is more like literary or legal interpretation than physics or chemistry.[3]

In this way Dilthey squarely challenged the claim of science to be the paradigm of all knowledge including that of the human world. There was no need to make the human studies more rigorous by squeezing them into the mould of the scientific methods because they had a tradition of their own to look back to, a tradition as old and as much concerned with the discovery of truth as that of the sciences. Not that Dilthey—as should be clear already—envisaged hermeneutics as an exclusive alternative to the scientific method; because man was not pure mind a combination of methods was usually required. But hermeneutics is important as the methodology for studying the most distinctive features of the human world.

Dilthey's conviction that our conception of the subject must govern the methods of studying it determines his methodology of the human studies. We have already seen how he developed his conception of man as the creature who is capable of perceiving meaning in his life, of expressing it in a multitude of ways, and so creating a whole world of objective mind which only he can understand. These outstanding features of human life, clarified in a philosophic anthropology, were intended as the general framework of Dilthey's methodology. But, to fulfil what he considered the aims of a methodology, he supplemented the broad outlines of his approach with a number of principles which embodied general lessons learned in the tradition of past research, and spelled out further features of human life which had a bearing on methodology.

I shall list five of his most important principles, numbered for convenience. The first is that individual cases are intrinsically interesting as subjects of the human studies. Speaking, in this case, of history, he said, 'In this universe of moral forces the unique and the individual has a different meaning from the one it has in outer nature. To understand it is not a means but an end in itself' (Vol. I, p.91). Obviously the physicist is also concerned with particular objects, for example, iron filings when studying magnetism, but his aim is to arrive at generalizations or to test a theory and, once he has done so, he ceases to be interested in those particular bits of metal. In the human studies we do not always aim for high-level generalizations and, even when we try to achieve them, they do not eclipse our interest in the material on which they are based. So Goethe's description of his visual imagination, Freud's self-analysis or Margaret Mead's account of growing up in Samoa, remain of absorbing interest whether the theories based on them are established or not. Indeed, if the social sciences had been only, or even mainly, concerned with the universal nature of society, religion or art we would have to admit that their conclusions are meagre, commonplace and uninteresting and their success unimpressive. Instead, they have thrown light on particular societies, family relationships in a particular civilization, town or even village, and the form certain institutions have taken at a specific time and place because the normal objects of understanding are individual entities. What we usually try to understand is a poem, not poetry, an action, not action in general; we look at individual expressions or their creators either of which may be as complex and composite as a whole code of law or a civilization. It would be difficult and unprofitable to generalize from such particular cases because their differences are just as important as their similarities and are due to their historical character. There is little to be said about '*the* family' or '*the* state' compared with what can be discovered about a state or family in a particular place or at a particular stage of their development.

Individual human beings have pride of place for Dilthey regarded them as natural units in a stronger sense than the parts of which they are made up (organs, cells or molecules) or the larger wholes (families or societies) of which they are part. They can think, feel and strive, so they are the real subject-matter of the human studies; they are capable of having their own point of view, so they can never lose their interest for the researcher or their claim to moral consideration. Hence Dilthey's first principle that individual cases are intrinsically interesting to the human studies challenges the emphasis on general laws noticeable within science.

Dilthey's second methodological principle postulates the importance of explanations in terms of parts and wholes within the human sphere. It is closely linked to the first because, unlike its theoretical alternative—explaining things in terms of general laws—it keeps attention focussed on individual objects. If, for example, we describe someone as a wealthy South American we are attributing to him features he shares with others, but when we say that his left leg is shorter than his right, that his heart rules his head, that he is my brother-in-law or the chairman of the local Round Table we are referring to relationships within him, or between him and other individual entities, which make up his identity as an individual.

This type of explanation is not the monopoly of the human studies nor their only method but it plays a larger part in them than in the sciences. Part–whole explanations can and must be given about physical things just as generalizations must be involved in explaining human phenomena. Examining how pistons and cylinders are related in an engine is like analysing the structure of a poem—the rules of grammar or prosody have their counterparts in the laws of physics. The distinction lies in the degree to which one explanation or the other is prominent.

The two forms of explanation are, clearly, interdependent. To explain the movement of the earth one cannot dispense with the law of gravity nor with the knowledge of the earth's position relative to the sun; in the same way, understanding a personal relationship involves knowing about human nature in general and the persons involved in particular. It remains true, however, that part–whole relationships are particularly important and prominent in the human studies. Each individual is part of a family, families are parts of a larger community, communities and associations make up a society; similarly, words are used in sentences, and actions are usually part of a purposive chain of actions. All these relationships are much more significant than those of a grain of sand to its heap or a blade of grass to the lawn, because they affect the very nature of the objects (i.e. a word may have a different meaning in different sentences). The fact that the units with which the human studies deal are both wholes consisting of parts and parts of larger wholes (or wider contexts) also produces a hierarchical order which suggests further lines along which research can be deepened or widened. Finally, the constituents of the world of mind have further characteristics—they can be part of several contexts at the same time and, indeed, form their crossing-points. For example, a speech may be a characteristic, psychological manifestation and a contribution to a political debate, so that an individual's life and the nation's politics may touch at that point. These webs of contextual relations indicate how we can gain understanding and achieve explanations which makes the part–whole relationship methodologically important.

Dilthey's third methodological principle is that we must start from the level of complexity which we encounter in actual experience. It was prompted by Dilthey's empiricism and we have already mentioned his reasons for adopting it when we considered this aspect of his philosophy in Chapter 4. This is how Dilthey himself applies it to psychology. 'Psychology must start from developed mental life and not deduce it from elementary processes' (Vol. V, p.168–9).[4] Again and again, but particularly in his writings on psychology, Dilthey recommended giving painstaking descriptions of complex states and events and analysing them in terms of their context; in his essays and biographical sketches he practised what he preached. Instead of discussing the poet's imagination in terms of simple processes observed in animals and small children or deduced from general assumptions, he turned to the testimony of great writers. This same principle led Dilthey to reject the idea of man as an isolated biological unit rather than a socially and culturally moulded being.

(To avoid misunderstanding it should be added that Dilthey did not reject or despise methods which built up the complex from the simple. He only claimed that they were insufficient by themselves and must be supplemented by, and indeed take second place to, the method he recommended.)

Dilthey's fourth methodological principle derives directly from his rejection of any absolute starting-point and asserts that any search for knowledge is involved in a kind of circle. It applies universally and on all levels, and we have already encountered some of its applications; we must understand the words to understand the sentence yet only by understanding the sentence can we properly understand the words; to learn what a social group is like we must learn about the individuals who compose it but their nature is moulded by being part of the group. This same circular interdependence links different disciplines like psychology and sociology, history and anthropology, philosophy and the empirical studies of man. This oscillating movement between different points of view which gradually leads to clarification bears some resemblance to the dialectical process as defined by Hegel and Marx. Dilthey did not describe it in this way, probably because he thought that was too formal for what he conceived to be a very varied and flexible process. In my view, what Dilthey had in mind is best described as a shuttlecock movement.

Dilthey's fifth and last principle might be called the double-focus principle. Basically it takes two forms of which the second is a specification and expansion of the first. Its first form may be put as follows: man must be considered as both an object and a subject. As an object he is the product or creature to be explained in terms of the circumstances which made him what he is; as a subject he must be understood as the being who knows himself, creates his environment and controls his actions. 'The individual is simultaneously an element in the interaction of society—a crossing-point of the various systems of interaction who consciously and deliberately reacts to their influence—and also a contemplating and investigating intelligence' (Vol. IV, p.63).[5] So we can study human behaviour systematically and explain it in casual terms, but must at the same time recognize that it is creative and produces new possibilities in history (rather than a predestined—and therefore, at least theoretically, predictable—pattern). This coloured his whole methodological approach for, valid though the scientific approach is within its own sphere, it is limited by the fact that the creative factors in human life can only be grasped by entering into the mental processes of creation, i.e. by understanding them and interpreting their products. To accept that man is both creature and creator is one way of saying that scientific and hermeneutic approaches must supplement each other in the study of man.

The second form of the principle stresses that in the human studies any interpretation must take into account the interpreter's point of view and that of the subject to be interpreted. It derives from the first formulation because it is based on the assumption that the subject-matter is (or is the product of) a creative consciousness with a point of view of its own. It could also be said that the social scientist's world is always an interpreted one so that he has no choice but to produce interpretations of interpretations. That the human studies involve conscious beings, each with ideas of his own, examining each other, is a familiar fact, but we may not have given sufficient methodological consideration to its implications.[6]

Dilthey was particularly interested in the application of this principle to history, to the problem of how the historian of one age can understand the actions of another. He wanted to eliminate disturbing factors and recapture the spirit of the original period. 'We must read the author without obstacle but also enjoy the historical and personal quality of his own mind. Hence everything which disturbs the calm, untroubled and clear flow of comprehension must be ruthlessly eliminated but everything unique which can be enjoyed without disturbance must be retained as a reflection of its inner historical form' (Letters to York, November 1896, p.226). There can be no formula for the balancing act involved; we must eliminate such obstacles to communication as metaphors or cross-references which no longer have any meaning for us and at the same time try to appreciate the particular flavour of these ideas which reflect his temperament and the spirit of his age. We must build bridges between ourselves and an author remote in time and yet keep him at a distance. We cannot, for instance, understand Plato properly, either by treating him as if he were a contemporary or as if he were historical phenomenon which has no relevance for us.

It is just as important as being judiciously faithful to the original to bring our own point of view, and what we know by hindsight, to bear on our interpretations.

States and rulers pursue their purposes conditioned by the horizons of their age; they act for themselves, not for the whole of history. But the significance of their acts in the context of history goes beyond the purposes they set themselves and only becomes visible to later ages. There is nothing mysterious about this; one need not trouble providence, nor attribute to history a purpose which it pursues on its own. In the wider contexts of passing time the consequences of purposes pursued become visible and make them appear as links in one single context which will, perhaps, merge into an even wider one later. (Vol. VII, p.341)[7]

An important consequence follows from this principle; because both imaginative insight into the minds of others and interpretations of one's own are involved, knowledge of the human world can never be a kind of photograph of reality. It is a construction (Dilthey called it the second world of mind) which our interpretations place on an original interpreted world (the first world of mind).

The order of concepts through which experiences come to be known originates only through the work of the mind which creates a *second* world of mind; this is based on the first but is created by the mind's tools—understanding, judging and thinking conceptually.

The history of the human studies shows, and logical, epistemological, reflection makes clear, that the historical representation of what has happened like the study of law or religion cannot, and cannot hope to be, a copy of recorded events. It is a new mental creation, rooted in the conditions of knowledge. (Vol. VII, p.307)[7]

Through this interplay of the first and second worlds of mind human life as a whole becomes meaningful.

This is the orderly progression in which the particular, outwardly conditioned, manifold of circumstances is adjusted to the mind's goals. It is an orderly progression because the circumstances are retained in it but in a higher form of consciousness. What is accidental becomes part of a context free from accident and from any external influence or internal association; what is particular becomes part of a whole or an example of something general; the image is submerged in the object and the concept, feeling, in value; from the experience of willing, norms arise and obscure strivings are clarified into purposes. The flow of life in which everything becomes part of the past is overcome by memory and the accidental nature of events by the context of thought. (Vol. VII, p.329)[7]

In this description of how the natural world is culturally transformed we see one of the implications of the double-focus principle.

To these five principles Dilthey added methodological guidelines derived from a number of ideas about human nature with which he filled in the broad outlines we have already discussed. He started by underlining the obvious but sometimes neglected or deliberately ignored fact that man is a psycho-physical being, an animal which thinks, a body endowed with mind. 'Because man is a psycho-physical whole, history consists of human actions, i.e. of physical behaviour, accompanied by mental content' (Vol. XVIII, p.103). Because man is an animal Dilthey considered it important to study his reactions to other animals in the evolutionary scale and to develop knowledge about his brain, nerves and glands. Because he is also part of the world of mind, the study of his religions, philosophies and literary creations is equally important. But, while some investigations can concentrate squarely on either the mental or the physical aspect of human nature, others have to face man's dual nature. It is reasonable to assume—as Dilthey, following in the footsteps of distinguished predecessors, undoubtedly did—that man's posture, the position of his thumb, the size of his brain and the nature of his vocal cords have something to do with his capacity for producing culture and may even account for some of its features. It was equally obvious to Dilthey that our natural functions and instinctive propensities are transformed within cultural contexts. Though there is nothing more clearly based on physiological features than eating and sleeping, there are enormous cultural variations in what we eat or when we sleep.

So much is clear enough but the methodological problem is to keep both aspects of man in sight and devise ways of bringing them meaningfully to bear on each other. It is quite likely, for instance, that evidence about the violence of overcrowded monkeys throws light on urban aggression because it is reasonable to assume that our responses resemble those of a closely related species. Dilthey himself would have been keenly and sympathetically interested in such research. But—as he would also have stressed—even more foolish than rejecting this line of approach would be to treat it as the only avenue to explanation. Unlike monkeys, we watch television, form political associations, worry about unemployment and believe in various things. Factors like these must be equally relevant and modify whatever tendencies we share with the monkeys.

When Dilthey looked at the relationship between mind and matter he saw the mind as an 'interpolation in the great text of nature'. It has been developed by a particular creature in the course of evolution and modifies his natural behaviour. But Dilthey considered more often and systematically the role of physical factors in the context of the world of mind. From this point of view he saw the body, and matter generally, as a means used by the mind to express itself and realize its aims. We use our speech organs to communicate ideas and our limbs to execute our purposes and, in an analogous way, we employ a variety of things as tools and materials. (Students of continental philosophy will recall that this idea of outer nature as a set of tools recurs dramatically in Heidegger's philosophy.) We adjust our bodies and external objects to our purposes but, in doing so, we also discover that we have to adjust our plans to the means available and that our actions generally are conditioned by external factors. Dilthey, therefore, saw the material world as the conditions which circumscribe our lives. The characteristic architecture or sculpture of a civilization, for instance, is shaped as much by the availability of wood or marble, the climate and landscape as by the imagination of the creator or the development of theories. So the human studies must systematically take into account the whole physical environment insofar as it limits choices or extends opportunities and facilitates particular actions. Psychology must consider our physiological make-up and history such hard facts as climate and geographical features. Understanding the course of a battle, to give one of Dilthey's own illustrations, requires not only knowledge of the general's plan and the soldiers' morale, but also of the terrain and the firepower of guns. A country's economy is not only governed by five-year plans but by floods and droughts.

Though these are essentially common-sense points, Dilthey thought them worth making because they underline the importance of relating the human studies systematically to such disciplines as physiology, geography or physical anthropology. He did not intend to isolate the human studies and here his conception of the interdependence of different disciplines, and even groups of disciplines, comes into its own. On the strictly methodological level the main question is how to combine a hermeneutic with a scientific approach.

The second methodologically significant human characteristic is that man's individual characteristics are socially and culturally conditioned. So, just as we must relate the study of man's physical and mental characteristics, so we must combine examination of individual psychological processes with investigation of the social and cultural forces which transform them. Psychology and Sociology must be treated as interdependent and this must influence the procedures of both disciplines. 'Man as a fact preceding history and society is a fiction of genetic explanation; the subject matter of a sound, analytical, science is individual man as a constituent of society' (Vol. I, p.31). Dilthey put this even more strongly in Volume IV (p.60):[8] 'It is a false individualism which extracts individuals from the social interaction of which they are elements and equips them with innate instincts. No exact psychology can at present justify an assumption which so far transcends the range of our experience and undertakes to construe the original constitution of an isolated individual who, after all, does not exist anywhere.'

Students of the social sciences will appreciate that this is not an abstruse academic point nor a matter of pedantically redrawing the frontiers between disciplines, but a live issue which is being debated by specialists to this day. It took patient research to demonstrate that the work of some very eminent investigators was flawed because they took for manifestations of universal human nature what turned out to be the peculiarity of a particular group—say the Austrian middle-classes—among which they were working. A famous contribution to this continuing debate was Margaret Mead's work, in which she tried to show that some of the differences between male and female, previously considered to be innate, were in fact culturally conditioned.[9] Today the pendulum has begun to swing the other way and recent publications have tried to remind us of the importance of physiologically determined differences. It is a testimony to the fruitfulness of Dilthey's approach that he anticipated issues of this type—in fact this very issue.

In our culture the fundamental difference lies in the fact that women's emotional and intellectual life arises from close, personal relationships to family, husband and child while vocational training makes men see life in terms of more objective and comprehensive, but also less immediate and personal, relationships. How much of these differences is the consequence of upbringing, how much of unalterable, fixed endowments can only be gradually answered by educational experiments. (Vol. IV, p.236)[10]

The third methodologically significant characteristic of man is that his nature has both immutable and historically determined features. He has fixed traits which systematic disciplines like psychology can study but is also a historical being. History, therefore, must use the systematic disciplines while all these disciplines must use historical material and apply concepts which reflect man's mutability in time. This is why history and the systematic disciplines are involved in a hermeneutic circle. Psychology, for example, must aid history, but can do so only when it is already enriched by historical material. 'Psychological certainties are insufficient for an explanation of the deepest manifestations of the human mind; a combination of psychological description and analysis with the dissection of historical facts promises to provide the basis of a psychology of contents which alone can serve history' (Vol. VIII, p.15).[11]

Psychology must use historical material because indirect knowledge, i.e. knowledge not gleaned directly from the observation of human behaviour but from examining its products, is most important. Dilthey always insisted that it is man's creations which reveal most clearly what he is. 'Psychology possesses firm and enduring material in the uniformity of individual human products, in the great and pervasive contexts which link these products into cultural systems and in the persistence of powerful organisations which unite people and rest on natural kinship; this makes a real analysis of man's mental life, even as regards its fundamental content, possible' (Vol. V, p.226).[12] But, as we have already learned, all this material does not consist of hard facts because it is the product of historical interpretations which have been coloured by the interpreter's point of view and valuations. 'What has happened and what is happening, the unique, accidental and momentary, is referred back to a value-charged and meaningful context . . . one can then understand how the outlook and horizon of an age are always the presuppositions for the particular way in which that age sees the historical world' (Vol. VII, pp.3–4).[13]

It would be possible to examine Dilthey's methodology in greater detail—particularly interesting would be to pursue further than I have done in Chapter 3 the use he made of his methodological principles. But this brief account of the different principles and guidelines, together with the quotations illustrating them, should be sufficient to indicate his main conclusions. Starting with a strong sense of the interdependence of all knowledge which makes common methods and interdisciplinary cooperation important, he yet felt it necessary to treat the human studies as a separate group of disciplines which, because of the nature of their subject-matter, require a distinct methodology—hermeneutics. This approach he spelled out in terms of principles about the importance of the individual, the need for part–whole explanations, the danger of side-stepping complex issues at the outset, the circularity of all inquiries and the necessity for a double focus on man. From his general conception of man he derived not only the broad outlines of his whole methodology, but also specific guidelines related to such facts as that man is both a physical and spiritual being, an individual and a social creature, unchanging subject and changing object of history.

There are undoubtedly gaps in Dilthey's exposition. One wishes that he had explained his views on the relationship between hermeneutics and the scientific method in greater detail and discussed the connection between different types of explanations more fully. An enlarged and more cogent exposition of his theory of the categories of life and of his philosophy of language would have made the basis of his methodology clearer. Nonetheless, his contribution has been more comprehensive, more balanced and more searching, than that of any other theoretician of the human studies. By now some of his ideas have become commonplace (which is frequently the fate of successful innovators); others may yet prove their fruitfulness if taken up seriously. Even some of the loose ends he left in his deliberately tentative theories still prove stimulating. After all, methodologies must not be judged by their neatness as theories but by their power to draw attention to vital issues.

In conclusion it may be worth while to remind ourselves of the purposes served by Dilthey's methodology. He valued knowledge for its own sake because he considered man's understanding of himself important, but he never tired of insisting that knowledge must be practical and guide action, though this must not be conceived in narrow, utilitarian terms. To appreciate its full range one must see it as answering these three questions: What is likely? What is possible? What is desirable? The social sciences try to answer the first question not only in order to satisfy our natural curiosity, or even anxiety, about the future but also to test their theories through their predictive value, and the second question to prove their practical usefulness by showing how we can achieve our aims. But, if the human studies were confined to these narrow, utilitarian aims they would always serve whatever purposes were set for them—crime prevention or robbery, subversion or conformity, revolution or reaction. When Dilthey claimed that the human studies must, and can, also answer the third question he expressed his conviction that the human studies can help us to clarify our values and crystallize our aims by showing what man was and is, what ideas he treasures and what traditions he has developed. Understanding ourselves teaches us how we should live. This is not a purely factual matter so here the empirical human studies must cooperate with philosophy.

Dilthey's full programme can only be accomplished by the study of man with 'philosophic intent'.[14]

11

Dilthey's influence

At the beginning I claimed that Dilthey's thought was alive today and relevant to our own problems and their solutions. So I have presented his ideas, as far as possible, in such a way that students of the various spheres of modern thought could recognize the links. Now that the systematic exposition of Dilthey's ideas is before the reader it may be worth while to spell out his influence more explicitly. Sometimes this is easy and straightforward. One can list friends and disciples, editors and expositors of his writings. These, naturally, were mostly German philosophers, psychologists, educationalists and literary historians who became influential in the '30s and '40s and are now dead. They were the main channel through which Dilthey's influence has reached us, but are only of specialist interest.

If we cast our net a little wider we come to thinkers like Husserl and Heidegger who, without being his followers, have praised his ideas and acknowledged his influence, thinkers who themselves became enormously influential. The difficulty in such cases is to decide how great their debt is. Original thinkers often distort what they appropriate, exaggerate how much they differ from those they are most indebted to and forget, or underplay, the extent of their borrowing.

But a thinker is not really influential if one can list all the people he affected. His ideas must have become part of the intellectual climate, which means that the connections have become untraceable and we must be on our guard against crowing over every accidental similarity of thought or phrasing. Tracing possible connections can be very fascinating, but here something much simpler is not only sufficient but more important—to consider the relation of Dilthey's ideas, irrespective of their precise origin, to our own. This is what really matters, though influences and acknowledgements of indebtedness, where they are clear, are worth mentioning.

In my view Dilthey has produced the most coherent, comprehensive, searching and fruitful philosophy of the human studies in the history of thought. So many thinkers on this subject since his time are following in his wake. Unfortunately certain obvious weaknesses in his work obscured and confused the precise nature of his influence. Dilthey's writings, scattered over thousands of pages (and trickling out into print for over a hundred years) are incomplete and not fully systematized; moreover some of his most interesting ideas are only expressed in unrevised fragments. His arguments are not as incisive and cogent as those of other great philosophers and some of his views, such as those on moral philosophy, remain highly controversial; thus stereotyped views have come to be associated with his name. Dilthey was *not* committed to a purely psychological approach, he did *not* advocate understanding at the expense of other cognitive approaches, and he did *not* accept complete historical relativity.

Dilthey's searching and comprehensive approach took account not only of the whole range of problems in the social sciences of his time but also anticipated those which their further development encountered. He became aware of, and advocated, the increased use of statistics in the social sciences, and speculated on the light which mental illnesses can throw on the normal functioning of the mind. He saw the need for typologies in the study of personality and by his theory of expressions, provided a framework for the kind of theory Freud was to develop. The relevance of literature for psychology and the interdependence between history and sociology were among other matters which occupied his mind. The main point here is not the width of his knowledge, his inventiveness or sensitivity to new ideas, but the fact that all these ideas fell into place within a comprehensive scheme.

Today we have scientists who understand the use of statistics infinitely better than Dilthey. Freud and his disciples elaborated a theory which went far beyond Dilthey's elementary reflections.

Men such as Max Weber translated Dilthey's hunches about the link between history and sociology into monumental works and one could go on through other ideas of Dilthey's mentioned above or referred to earlier. But the question is: have we, as yet, achieved an intellectual grasp which can span the use of statistical tests, animal studies, psychoanalysis, history, sociology and literary criticism? More and more scholars have become aware that they cannot profitably pursue their different lines of approach towards the understanding of man without taking notice of each other's work. Once they began to reflect on the bearing these different approaches have on each other, to consider their respective merits and drawbacks and ask what their combined conclusions imply about man's nature and destiny they encountered Dilthey's enormous shadow. If they come at first or second hand across his ideas they welcome them as a basis for their own reflections. But they may, even unknowingly, be driven, by the nature of their subject-matter, into the pattern of thought first sketched out by Dilthey.

Three areas of his influence merit particular attention; the impact of his ideas within philosophy itself and the role which his epistemological and methodological theories played in the development of both psychology and sociology. Before expanding on these it is important to mention two further respects in which he affected the intellectual climate—the lead he gave to the history of ideas and to interdisciplinary cooperation.

By arguing that history received its meaning from the ideas of the actors involved in the historical process, Dilthey focussed attention on the importance of the history of ideas. According to his argument it was not just one specialised branch of history like the history of hairdressing, but an integral part and essential clue to all history. As he considered history to be the royal highroad to the solution of most problems the history of ideas thus became a very important subject. Since Dilthey practised this discipline with zeal and distinction many scholars have followed in his footsteps and today it is hardly necessary to document the popularity of the subject, which ranges from attempts to account for the ebb and flow of civilizations by analysing, like Spengler and Toynbee, their religious and moral ideas, to the innumerable histories of special bodies of ideas, such

165

as the history of art, the history of science and the history of historiography. It is also noteworthy that fairly recently degree courses on the history of ideas have been developed in British universities.

Dilthey's broad, non-specialist, even interdisciplinary approach is clearly not new; on the contrary increasing specialization is the newcomer. Polymaths, like Dilthey and Max Weber, are the last to follow in a tradition now smothered by the sheer weight of knowledge. It was never easy to be really knowledgeable in several disciplines; now it is almost impossible, though the theoretical framework which Dilthey created can make cooperation between experts meaningful and fruitful. His philosophy makes it clear that the different disciplines belong together and are not isolated kingdoms each with its own territory. Areas of human activity, say management or delinquency, are not just the province of a particular discipline but have psychological, sociological and economic dimensions. There is now an increasing recognition that coordinating these different lines of approach cannot be left to the accident of one man with knowledge of several disciplines, or several men whose offices are in the same building. Points of view embodied in particular disciplines are interdependent and can be correlated in a particular investigation. By analyzing the nature of the human world and the way different disciplines single out different aspects of it, Dilthey provided guidelines for such an approach. Today such interdisciplinary approaches are becoming more and more fashionable, and recognized as theoretically respectable and practically valuable. Here Dilthey's ideas, because they helped to provide the original impulse for this whole trend, may help us to spell out the philosophic foundations of this approach.

Dilthey's philosophy had its most immediate effect on his own friends and disciples, but as even the most distinguished of them like E. Spranger and G. Misch are not widely known in the English-speaking world it is not worth expanding on this aspect of his influence. He also influenced other thinkers of world-wide reputation but perhaps not so extensively as his friends. One of these was Husserl. Quaintly referring to himself in the third person he wrote to Misch on 27 June 1929:

The Dilthey–Heidegger confrontation concerns me, too, because it implies one between Dilthey and Husserl. You do not know that a few conversations with Dilthey in Berlin in 1905 (not his writings) stimulated the Husserl of the *Logical Investigations* so that he became the Husserl of the *Ideas*; the phenomenology of ideas, incompletely described then and really only completed between 1913 and 1925 agrees intimately with Dilthey—though the method is quite different.[1]

Without going into details one can appreciate that the shift to which Husserl refers is one towards a greater awareness of historical perspectives, of the empirical world and of the relevance of philosophy to its problems.[2]

It is hardly necessary to document the growing influence of Husserl's ideas (and through them those of Dilthey). He has found distinguished expositors in the Anglo-Saxon world[3] and affinities between his work and that of the linguistic analysts have been discovered.[4] Indeed the influence of phenomenology —the usual name for his philosophy—has extended beyond philosophy into psychology and sociology where it has become a rallying point for movements which rejected positivist approaches (i.e. attempts to make the social sciences as much as possible like other sciences). Ethnomethodology is one of these recent manifestations; having penetrated its eccentric terminology (which extends to its name) one recognizes ideas already advocated by Dilthey and Husserl.[5]

As well known and as influential as Husserl is Heidegger, who explicitly knowledged Dilthey's influence. He picked out, powerfully emphasized and incisively wove together three themes which had lain buried in Dilthey's scattered and partly unpublished works (though this is not all that Heidegger did). The first theme is the need for a basic philosophic analysis of the crucial characteristics of human existence which alone can provide the key to knowledge of any kind; second is the outstanding importance of temporal perspectives, of man's 'historicity', which is why Heidegger called his main work *Being and Time*. His third theme was the exclusive emphasis on the hermeneutic method.

These three themes have claimed increasing attention apart from, and after the decline of, existentialism. Philosophic anthropology has been put on the map as a distinct discipline though it is often hard to decide how far its exponents have drawn their inspiration directly from Dilthey and how far they are indebted to existentialism.[6]

Emphasis on historical perspectives has become a major feature of the intellectual scene which makes it all the more difficult to decide where Dilthey's influence was at work. He tried to provide philosophic foundations for an idea associated with the so-called historical school which he admired, namely that most things are subject to historical change and must, therefore, be explained historically. This historicism owes something to Hegel and its most widely known form is Marxism. Collingwood and Croce,[7] both of whom knew and admired Dilthey, are among the non-Marxist exponents of this point of view.

Hermeneutics, too, has been taken up increasingly in various areas of scholarship. The most sustained philosophic discussion of it is to be found in Gadamer's *Truth and Method*[8] but it has also been used by theologians and literary critics.[9] Quite recently A. Bullock reported that he had come across the term and that, being unable to understand it properly, had initiated a new reference book.[10]

Gadamer's explicit discussion of Dilthey's hermeneutics encouraged Habermas to examine it anew and use it in his polemics against positivism. He was a member of the Frankfurt school which brings us to another channel through which Dilthey's influence was transmitted.[11] This school was founded as an institute by a group of Marxist-orientated scholars during the Weimar republic. Exiled from Germany by the Nazis it spent the war years in New York and its leaders returned to Germany when hostilities ended. Outstanding members, such as Horkheimer, Adorno and, above all, Marcuse, temporary associates like E. Fromm and (from a younger generation) Habermas, have now become extremely well known. Many of their works are available in English and feature as textbooks in British and American Universities. Marcuse and Fromm were interviewed within weeks of each other on British Television early in 1978.

The philosophic orientation of the Frankfurt school was coloured by the personalities of its members and the historical situation in which they found themselves. As middle-class Jewish scholars they shared a profound interest in culture, especially in poetry, literature, music and the arts. Because of their circumstances they raised specific questions about the social and political processes which affected them. Why did fascism arise and gain so much support? Was the collapse of capitalism really as imminent as orthodox Marxists predicted? And was there, in consequence, a revolutionary situation? Was there a danger of incipient fascism in the Western democracies? How did mass culture and the mass media affect these different potential trends? While they considered these issues from a distinctly philosophic angle, they were not purely philosophers but worked on the history of ideas, sociology or psychology.

These cultural, social and psychological interests were not the only thing which diluted their Marxist orientation. They also realized that the orthodox Marxism of that time was unable to answer these questions convincingly just as the application of that Marxism in Russia had not, as they soon realized, produced the humane society they envisaged. On the other hand they found philosophical schools like logical positivism and the behaviouristic approach to the social sciences sterile. So they sympathized with the sense of practical commitment in Dilthey's philosophy. They shared his interest in cultural phenomena and appreciated his insistence on the value and interest of individuals. Hence they subscribed to and adapted methods which Dilthey had advocated and justified in his work. The most explicit theoretical expression of this trend comes in Habermas' use of Dilthey's ideas to combat positivism and to demonstrate the constructive functions of cultural criticism.

Finally, before I leave the subject of Dilthey's influence on philosophy, I must mention the Spanish thinker, Ortega y Gasset.[12] He not only acknowledged Dilthey's greatness and influence but also initiated a Spanish translation of Dilthey's work which is more comprehensive than anything available in English. His own writings bear a very striking resemblance to Dilthey's own ideas.

Dilthey's ideas on psychology also bore fruit or, to put it as cautiously as possible, anticipated and put into a systematic context, developments which have since proved their usefulness. Psychology, when Dilthey turned to it a hundred years ago, was in a fairly elementary state. To list some of Dilthey's ideas on the subject is almost enough to show how he affected subsequent development.

(1) Man is a psycho-physical being; therefore a balance between physiological studies, comparative studies of animal behaviour, and ecological studies, on the one hand, and an understanding of mental processes, on the other, is needed.

(2) The human mind functions as a structural whole which controls and modifies its individual mental activities.

(3) Mental life finds expression in a multitude of ways including facial expressions, gestures, postures and all kinds of behaviour.

(4) The products of human behaviour, i.e. the pictures men have painted, the letters they have written, the poems or stories they have composed, the institutions they have created, provide the most substantial basis for knowledge of human nature.

(5) The entities listed under (3) and (4) reveal more than their authors intended. Through them we may come to know what was not deliberately communicated and even what was not consciously present to their authors' minds.

(6) Man is a psycho-social being. We cannot understand individuals in isolation but only in the context of their social relations and in terms of the cultural influences to which they have been exposed.

(7) Man is a historical being. We cannot assume an unchanging human nature but must accept that the continuous, one-way process of historical change may make a difference to what man is at any particular period.

(8) Psychology cannot safely concentrate exclusively on simple phenomena such as sensations, instincts and reflexes, which can be isolated in experimental situations or stipulated by analogy to lower forms of life, in the hope that complex mental phenomena can be explained in terms of these elements. It must study complex phenomena like artistic creation or political choice.

(9) As well as theoretical explanations, and even for such explanations, a lot more detailed, searching description of complex, mental, phenomena and human behaviour is needed.

Some of these ideas have become commonplaces; that human behaviour can be interpreted as expressions of mental life, and even of unconscious motives, has been made familiar by Freud and his disciples. Today popular articles expand on this theme, telling us about the significance of habitual postures during sleep and the meaning of automatic gestures like crossing your legs or folding your arms. These go far beyond Dilthey in their wealth of detail but often lack his insight into methodological problems such as the difficulties of testing interpretations.

Other ideas of Dilthey's are still part of current controversies. Even today it is necessary for certain psychologists to protest that man's intellectual processes and decisions are not made much more comprehensible by studying the comparatively elementary thinking and choices made by rats or pigeons.

One interesting development in psychology very much in line with Dilthey's thinking is the inclusion of social and cultural factors in modern theories of personality. It must be clear from what has already been said that Dilthey saw personality as much more than the product of physiological urges, biological endowments or even the interaction within the family group. For him it was also shaped by tradition, cultural ideals and beliefs and had to be understood in these terms. A man may strive to be a scholar or a hero, a man of the world or a saint, a Casanova or a statesman and this shapes his personality. These ideals, in turn, change their content, become extinct or gain in popularity in different social and historical circumstances. Once, to be a gentleman had a precise meaning and meant a lot to men of a certain class; today some people regard it as a joke. A typology of personalities in terms of such culturally determined ideals was initiated by E. Spranger,[13] whom we have already mentioned as a philosophic disciple of Dilthey, but the same idea can be traced in some modern work on the psychology of personality.

Perhaps the best known single work based on such a cultural typology comes from the Frankfurt school. It is the *Authoritarian Personality*—produced by Adorno and some of his colleagues.[14] We have already seen that the members of the Frankfurt school were interested in the origins of fascism and the danger of it spreading to other countries. They worked on the hypothesis that fascism might encourage and, in turn, be supported by a certain type of personality sympathetic to fascism, namely the 'authoritarian' personality. So they asked themselves what the main

171

characteristics of such a personality were and how these could be identified; they wondered about the circumstances which produced such personalities. Using a combination of questionnaires, interviews and tests the group of investigators showed that there were positive correlations between a number of attitudes, such as racialism, militarism and status anxiety and that these attitudes and their relations to each other were the products of a certain kind of upbringing and family situation. They were also determined, as became increasingly clear, by social, political and historical factors. For instance, otherwise similar personalities may turn out to be left wing or right wing under slightly different cultural circumstances.

This piece of research has proved highly influential because, quite apart from its conclusions, it was original in its interdisciplinary approach and in the methodological assumptions it made. It should be clear how much this owes to Dilthey's spirit. The need to enter into, i.e. to understand the meaning of, particular attitudes is fully recognized and so is the importance of going beyond the individual responses to the cultural context (or sphere of objective mind) which determined these responses and through which alone they can be understood. Put crudely—to understand fascists it is not enough to elicit responses from individual fascists one must also read standard fascist literature. T. Adorno put this point vigorously, though in his usual obscure language:

It appeared to me, and I am still persuaded today, that in the cultural sphere what is regarded by the psychology of perception as a mere 'stimulus' is, in fact, qualitatively determined, a matter of 'objective spirit' and knowable in its objectivity. I oppose stating and measuring effects without relating them to these 'stimuli' i.e. the objective content to which the consumers in the cultural industry, the radio listeners, react. . . . To proceed from the subjects' reactions, as if they were a primary and final source of sociological knowledge seems to me thoroughly superficial and misguided.[15]

Dilthey's influence on sociology via phenomenology has already been mentioned. It must also be clear by now that the use which the Frankfurt school, and Habermas in particular, made of Dilthey's ideas has affected their work in sociology and their reflections on its methodology. (Like Dilthey the members of this school all shared wide interests which extended to sociology and an interdisciplinary approach.) But the pivotal point in considering the role which Dilthey's philosophy plays in sociology is the extent to which it influenced Max Weber. It is hardly necessary to argue that the combination of methodological principles elaborated in Weber's work is one of the most powerful influences on modern sociology. How far are these Dilthey's ideas? There is no doubt that Weber was influenced by his thought and derived some ideas from him. Prominent among these, according to most commentators, is the concept of 'understanding' as the grasping of the subjective meaning or intention behind men's actions. But is this the only point of contact between these two thinkers? Certainly some writers on Weber have thought so, particularly those like Runciman,[16] who considered this conception of understanding Dilthey's sole and unqualified contribution to thought. But was it all that Weber knew about Dilthey's ideas? It is true that when Weber produced his works Dilthey's main philosophic ideas were still unpublished or buried in obscure proceedings or periodicals. But Weber was a young man in Berlin when Dilthey lectured there and in Heidelberg Troeltsch, who was undoubtedly influenced by Dilthey, was Weber's close friend. In the absence of further detective work I can only list some parallels in the thinking of these two men and leave readers to judge for themselves.

Influenced by the positivism he had encountered in such men as Mill, Dilthey was throughout his life profoundly pre-occupied with the problem of how understanding could be made objective, i.e. subject to testing and verification. In this he differed from the way the existentialists adapted hermeneutics to their use. This corresponds closely to the motive behind Weber's attempt to relate understanding to casual explanation, though Dilthey did not anticipate this particular solution, and would not have agreed with it.

Though he did not use the term 'ideal type', Dilthey frequently referred to the need for typologies in the human studies. It was the best that could be achieved in a field in which the importance and uniqueness of individual cases made generalizations and the establishment of general laws impossible.

Both men shared interest in, and stress, the importance of history. Both were concerned with understanding civilizations as a whole and used varied material, including literary sources for this purpose.

One of the striking features of Weber's approach is his use of texts, such as the writings of Benjamin Franklin and the *Westminster Confession*, to bring out the 'spirit of capitalism' or the essence of protestantism. Commentators on Weber have discussed this point illuminatingly and have stressed that modern sociology may yet have something to learn from this approach,[17] but less attention has been given to the fact that this is, indeed, the hermeneutic approach as advocated by Dilthey and rests on the kind of presuppositions he had spelled out. Among the most important of these are that units, such as ages or civilizations, have common features, that these find expression in objectifications such as literature or philosophy and that a systematic interpretation of these manifestations can therefore help us to understand these common features.

Finally, it is worth re-emphazising that Dilthey was not only concerned with the empathetic understanding of individuals but with the 'systematic, structural, analysis of the dynamic of human-social existence' to use one of the phrases which Landgrebe applied to his work. I should have thought this was also to be found in Weber's work.[18]

This does not amount to a claim that Weber slavishly followed Dilthey. Not only was he an original thinker but he was, unquestionably, influenced by a whole climate of opinion shaped by many thinkers among whom Rickert is considered to be particularly important. It is arguable, however, that some of the obscurities and ambiguities of Weber's thought can be eliminated by relating them to the context of Dilthey's more deliberately and systematically philosophic approach.

Once we have added Weber's to the other works through which Dilthey influenced modern sociology and mentioned in addition the impact which the growth of the history of ideas made on modern thought we need not be surprised about the many echoes of Dilthey's ideas we find in contemporary sociological literature.

Human beings must be understood as conscious beings with

purposes and points of view of their own. As J.F. Glass[19] put it,
' ... the proper study of human behaviour requires an intuition,
an empathy, an awareness of the other as a person who places
meaning on his behaviour' or in F. Matson's words, ' ... we
cannot understand the behaviour of human beings in strictly
"behavioural" terms. If we wish to know the meaning of behaviour we must know the *meanings* of the behavers; to remain
outside his frame of experience is simply to remain in the dark'.[20]
The philosopher A. Ryan makes almost the same point when he
writes ' ... the important definition of the situation so far as the
validity of the explanation is concerned turns out to be the
definition accepted by the people concerned'.[21]

The sociologist F.W. Gouldner brings out very clearly the
conclusion which Dilthey had already drawn from the fact that
the sociologist interprets interpretations.

A systematic and dogged insistence upon seeing ourselves as we see
others would, I have suggested, transform not only our view of ourselves
but also our view of others. We would increasingly recognise the depth
of our kinship with those whom we study ... they could ... be seen
as brother sociologists, each attempting with varying degrees of skill,
energy and talent to understand social reality.[22]

Recognized too is Dilthey's principle of dealing with a subject
on the appropriate level of complexity and, therefore, taking
account of human purposes and the intricate ways in which we
pursue them. C.H. Turner makes this point in an attack on
different forms of reductionism.

What social science has done is banish human *purpose* from its universe
of discourse. Purpose and processes are destroyed in analysis and a
mathematical combination of the parts cannot bring them back ...
while life processes face forward towards greater complexity, variety
and higher synthesis, the vast majority of social scientists face backwards,
searching for the causes of present behaviour in a myriad of separate
incidents, group affiliations, economic conditions and economic roles.
The practice of analysis assumes that the primitive can explain the
complex, what von Bertalanffy called the 'ratomorphic fallacy'.[23]

Lucien Goldmann made the same point without its pessimistic

175

defensiveness: 'here [in the human sciences] the progress of knowledge proceeds, *not from the simple to the complex* but from the abstract to the concrete through continual oscillation between the whole and its parts.'[24] (Readers will not miss the typically Diltheyan reference to the part–whole relationships.)

Finally there is a renewal or continuation of Dilthey's insistence that social science must be based on a conception of man that takes account of the various dimensions through which alone man can be properly understood. This, it will be remembered is the object of a philosophic anthropology. Here on this very theme is D.H. Wrong:

I do not see how, at the level of theory, sociologists can fail to make assumptions about human nature. If our assumptions are left implicit we will inevitably presuppose a view of man that is tailor-made to our special needs; when our sociological theory over-stresses the stability and integration of society we will end up imagining that man is the disembodied, conscience-driven, status-seeking phantom of current theory.[25]

Central to contemporary debates, as it was to Dilthey's thinking, is the role the study of man should take in our orientation within the world. At one extreme it is assumed that facts about man and his social involvements are like any other facts, such as those about the chemical properties of substances or about the vegetation on the earth. They can be established empirically and objectively, no valuation is implied, and the botanist does not have to claim the superiority of roses over nettles. Once the facts are established they can be put to any use one may choose—to grow nettles or to destroy them. Scholars who see the human sciences in this light believe that they tell us nothing about right and wrong and can be put to any purpose, any kind of social engineering or manipulation of human nature. The social sciences according to them provide the means for whatever goals we derive from feelings or moral convictions, just as the physical sciences provide the tools for whatever we chose to do—to preserve life or destroy it, to build houses or concentration camps.

The ethos behind this conviction is the rigorous pursuit of truth, a desire for clean, sharp, logical, distinctions between what is and what ought to be and a hatred of ambiguities and obfuscations. The opposite view is held with as much, or even more, fervour and conviction; it challenges the scientific approach on its own ground by stressing the dangers of bias, the difficulty of experimenting with people and the complexity of the human world. It makes, however, a further claim which goes to the heart of the matter. When man studies himself this cannot be a purely factual inquiry but is bound to become part of a critical self-assessment. It is even arguable that this is the chief aim of the human studies. Modern psychological research is clearly not like the agonized self-questioning of the ancient saints; the analysis of sociologists and historians not like the pronouncements of prophets and sages, on their civilizations. But is the difference so profound? Perhaps it is only our spirit and style which has changed. A couple of quotations, picked from a large field, will illustrate the point. Tom Burns wrote: 'The practice of sociology is criticism: to criticize or to raise questions about claims and assumptions concerning the value or meaning of conduct and achievement.'[26] E. Shils put it even more strongly: 'Sociological analysis is a continuation in a contemporary idiom of the great efforts of the human mind to render judgment on man's vicissitudes on earth.'

If this view is right students of human nature are wittingly and deliberately, or unwittingly and reluctantly, placed in this position of passing judgment on man and society. When a scholar such as Riesman distinguishes inner-directed and outer-directed man, when Adorno and his colleagues contrast the authoritarian and the democratic personalities, when economists describe the functioning of capitalism or of state monopoly or sociologists the alienation of man in modern technological society, judgments are made explicitly or implied. A certain personality type is preferred, a particular form of society is justified or condemned, ideals and aspirations are depicted as dangerous and destructive or as healthy and promising. So the social scientist assumes the mantle of the sage and prophet and is praised or abused for being the conservative defender of the old order or a revolutionary subverting it.

The difficulty of this position is the logical status of the transition from 'is' to 'ought', from diagnosis to prescription.

However shrewdly psychologists or psychiatrists diagnose what goes on in people's minds it does not entitle them to suggest how they *should* live; whatever sociologists may discover about society does not justify them considering it right or wrong.

The fact is that most of us most of the time, and this certainly applies to social scientists, take certain valuations for granted: health is good and alienation bad, social harmony is superior to disharmony, kindness is better than unkindness, variety superior to monotony, freedom to strict control. Where the results appear to conflict with our expectations we use a terminological escape route. 'Ah', we say, 'this was not *real* kindness, *proper* justice, or *genuine* freedom.' Once this is granted then it seems to be a purely factual matter if a particular measure aids personal health and justice or minimises alienation.

So valuation becomes a purely personal matter, indistinguishable from prejudice. Once the destructive analyses of modern philosophy have demolished the claim of reason to penetrate to ultimate reality and only barely admitted the competence of reason in the sphere of science, moral guidance must be scientific or nothing. We want our social science to be rigorous and objective but we also want it to be practical, telling us not only how to do things but what to do. The attraction of Marxism, for example, and of a great deal of sociology is that they appear to offer both, but it is not the social scientist's job to provide an epistemological justification for the widely accepted claim that the two can be combined nor has his training usually equipped him to provide it. For Dilthey it was an issue to which he explicitly addressed himself and on which he brought his extensive knowledge of the history of philosophy and his critical acumen to bear. The conclusions he reached are the basis of, and are implied in, all his work.

For Dilthey all knowledge came from experience—science being only an extension and systemization of everyday experience. The claims of religion or metaphysics to derive moral principles from some insight into ultimate reality—be it through revelation or the use of speculative reason—cannot, therefore, be justified. What can be established is what people normally need for survival and contentment, what they feel about different matters and what they have aspired to. The history of man's ideas and beliefs, principles and goals is itself on record, as are the consequences of man's beliefs and actions. This is all we have to go on. Dilthey knew, of course, that we must guard against simple and direct conclusions. The fact that sheer power has so often triumphed in history does not make it right, nor does the fact that a lot of people have derived pleasure from it, justify adultery. This is where philosophy comes in. It cannot, if Dilthey is right, produce justifiable moral doctrines by speculation (just as it cannot establish a defensible picture of reality) but it provides the critical reflection which we must bring to bear on the complex totality of human experience if we are to derive guidance from it. This may not be intellectually satisfactory; it is not as neat as a logical syllogism or the extrapolation from a statistical table, but it may be all we can attain and it may be better than abandoning ourselves to irrationalism and scepticism.

Many contemporary social scientists, such as the members of the Frankfurt school and others already quoted, feel that they must draw moral conclusions from their empirical research because when they look at man's nature, his creations and actions, they find it difficult not to take moral and political problems into account. They need objective information and have learned that nothing less will do, but they cannot remain detached spectators where man's own conduct and fate is at issue. So the social scientist must become something of a philosopher or seek the help of one. Unfortunately he cannot get much cooperation from the exponents of some very influential schools of philosophy, partly because they are committed to the widely held belief that there can be no bridge between what is and what ought to be and partly because they believe that philosophy must confine itself to purely theoretical clarification.

Dilthey's philosophy, on the other hand, is most helpful to the social scientists concerned with moral issues. They found in him a man who believed that philosophy must be practical as well as theoretical and must enter into close partnership with the social sciences. They can also draw inspiration from the moral seriousness with which he stressed the importance of individuals. It is no wonder that so many contemporary scholars are following paths first mapped out by Dilthey.

Bibliography

A chronological table of all of Dilthey's writings, lists of hundreds of books and articles on Dilthey (mainly in German) and references to translations of his works in various languages are available in U. Hermann, *Bibliographie Wilhelm Dilthey* (Berlin/Basel 1969). R.A. Makkreel's *Dilthey, Philosopher of the Human Studies* (Princeton 1975) also contains a fairly full and up-to-date bibliography of books and articles on Dilthey.

DILTHEY'S WRITINGS

Only the general title and subject of each volume is given but not a breakdown of its content which can be found in H.P. Rickman, *Wilhelm Dilthey, Selected Writings* (Cambridge 1976), subsequently abbreviated as *SW*. Where I have quoted in the text from the collected works, the precise source is given in my footnotes. English translations are listed under the appropriate volume.

Vol. I   *Introduction to the Human Studies*
          Translations: Preface and pp.14–21 in *SW*.
Vol. II   *The World-view and the Analysis of Man during the Renaissance and Reformation*
Vol. III *Contributions to the History of the German Spirit*
Vol. IV⎱
Vol. V ⎰ *The History of the Young Hegel*
Vol.VI   *The World of Mind. Introduction to the Philosophy of Life*
          Translations from Vol. V:
              Ideas about a Descriptive and Analytical Psychology in *Descriptive Psychology and Historical Understanding* trans. R.M. Zaner.
              Also selected passages in *SW*.

181

The Origins of Hermeneutics in *SW*.
The Nature of Philosophy (Vol. V, pp.339–416) trans.
as *The Essence of Philosophy* in S.A. and W.T. Emery
(North Carolina 1955).

Vol. VII   *The Constitution of the Historical World in the Human
Studies*
Translation:
Selected passages (about a hundred pages in each case)
in H.P. Rickman, *Meaning in History* (London 1961)
and in *SW*.
*Understanding of Other Persons and their life-expres-
sions* (Vol. VII, pp.205–20), trans. J. Kuehl in *Theories
of History* (New York 1959), also translated in *Descriptive Psychology and Historical Understanding* by K.L.
Heiges.

Vol. VIII   *The Types of World-views and their Development in the
Metaphysical Systems*
Translations:
pp.75–118 in *Philosophy of Existence, Introduction to
Weltanschauungslehre* by W. Kluback and M.
Weinbaum.
Selected passages in *SW*.

Vol. IX   *Theory of Education*
Vol. X   *System of Ethics*
Vol. XI   *The Origin of Historical Consciousness*
Vol. XII   *Contributions to Prussian History*
Vol. XIII   (1 and 2) *The Life of Schleiermacher*
Translations: 2 chapters in *SW*
Vol. XIV   (1 and 2) *Schleiermacher's System as Philosophy and
Schleiermacher's System as Theology*
Vol. XV
Vol. XVI   } *Contributions to the History of Ideas of the Nineteenth
Century*
Vol. XVII
Vol. XVIII *The Science of Man, Society and History*

In preparation

Vol. XIX   *Introduction to the Human Studies* (drafts for Vol. II)
Vol. XX   *Logic*
Vol. XXI   *German Poetry and Music* (the fuller version of a collection
of essays published separately in 1957)

Vol. XXII *The Great Poetry of Imagination* (a collection of essays previously published separately in 1954)
Translations: Passages in *SW*.

Experience and Poetry (Leipzig and Berlin 1905)
Translations: Chapter on Goethe's imagination in *SW*.

Note: H.A. Hodges, *W. Dilthey, an Introduction* contains some fifty pages of translations comprising 29 separate passages mainly from Vols. I, V and VII.

SECONDARY LITERATURE *(in English only)*

Antoni, C. *From History to Sociology* (London 1962)

Aron, R. *German Sociology* (New York 1964)

Brock, W. *An Introduction to Contemporary German Philosophy* (Cambridge 1935)

Gadamer, H. *Truth and Method* (London 1970)

Gardiner, P. (ed.) *Theories of History* (New York 1959)

Habermas, J. *Knowledge and Human Interests* (London 1971)

Hodges, H.A. *W. Dilthey, an Introduction* (London 1944)

Hodges, H.A. *The Philosphy of W. Dilthey* (London 1952)

Hughes, H.S. *Consciousness and Society* (New York 1958)

Mandelbaum, M. *The Problem of Historical Knowledge* (New York, 1938)

Müller-Vollmer, K. *Towards a Phenomenological Theory of Literature, a Study of W. Dilthey's Poetik* (The Hague 1963)

Palmer, R.E. *Hermeneutics* (Evanston 1969)

Rickman, H.P. *Meaning in History* (London 1961)

Rickman, H.P. *Understanding and the Human Studies* (London 1967)

Rickman, H.P. *Wilhelm Dilthey, Selected Writings* (Cambridge 1976)

References

I have translated all the titles of Dilthey's own works as this creates no problem of tracing them in the collected works (referred to simply by volume number).

SW refers to *Wilhelm Dilthey, Selected Writings;* "*Archiv*" to *Archiv der Geschichte der Philosophie; Proceedings* to *Proceedings of the Prussian Academy of Science.*

Chapter 1. The importance of Dilthey

1 p.129 of *Concord and Liberty* (1946) quoted by Müller-Vollmer.
2 E. Fueter wrote in the *Schweitzerische Hochschulzeitung* (1963, Vol. 36, p.233), 'The Introduction to the Human Studies has a similar significance for the studies of man as Isaac Newton's *Philosophiae Principia Mathematica* (1683) has for the sciences . . .' (quoted by Sauerland, see Chapter 2, note 5).
3 This theme is taken up in the final chapter.
4 See bibliography and Chapter 2, note 5.
5 from one of the earlier drafts of his theories about the human studies, first published 1977 as Vol. XVIII which is entitled *The Disciplines Concerned with Man, Society and History.*
6 *Present-day Culture and Philosophy* (1898). Included in Vol. VIII and trans. in *SW.*
7 *Nachlass* refers to unpublished works in the Dilthey archives in Berlin and Göttingen.
8 Graf Paul York von Wartenburg was a descendant of the Prussian Field-marshal who played an important part in the Napoleonic wars. His grandson was executed as a leading conspirator against Hitler in 1944.
9 *Exchange of Letters between W. Dilthey and the Count Paul York von Wartenburg 1877–97,* ed. S. von Schulenburg (1923).
10 *Y.D.* refers to *The Young Dilthey* by Clara Misch. See below p.23.
11 See Chapter 3 pp.32f for further details.

185

12 This volume contains a collection of his writings and drafts on the 'philosophy of philosophy' (i.e. his typology of world-views).

13 From Elbert Hubbard's *A Thousand and One Epigrams*.

Chapter 2. Dilthey's writings and their reception

1 See next chapter for fuller details.

2 R. Buchwald, *Goethezeit and Gegenwart* (1949), p.318, quoted by Rodi (see Chapter 2, note 5).

3 Husserl's letter to G. Misch, 27 June 1929. Quoted in Misch's *Lebensphilosophie und Phenomenologie* (3rd ed., 1929).

4 *Sein um Zeit* (Being and Time)

5 L. Landgrebe, *Dilthey's Theorie der Geisteswissenschaften, Analyse ihrer Grundbegriffe* (1928); G. Misch, *Lebensphilosophie und Phenomenologie*.

6 F. Krausser in his *Kritik der endlichen Vernunft* (Frankfurt 1968) drew on unpublished material to show that Dilthey made a substantial contribution to the general philosophy of science and anticipated system analysis.

F. Rodi's *Morphologie und Hermeneutik* (Stuttgart 1969) is an interesting analysis of Dilthey's view on the relation between scientific and hermeneutic methods. It also contains a stimulating discussion of Dilthey's fluctuating reputation.

K. Sauerland's *Dilthey's Erlebnisbegriff* (Berlin/New York 1972) concentrates on the role which Dilthey's concept of 'an experience' played in literary criticism.

B. Peschken in his *Versuch einer germanistischen Ideologie-kritik* (Stuttgart 1972) examines Dilthey's view on literature, and on Goethe in particular, in the context of his political attitudes.

H. Johach in his *Handelnder Mensch und objektiver Geist* (Meisenheim 1974) uses unpublished material to show how far Dilthey contributed to, and anticipated, fundamental sociological themes.

H. Ineichen, *Erkenntnistheorie und geschichtlich-gesellschaftliche Welt* (Frankfurt 1974), a discussion of Dilthey's indebtedness to Kant.

C. Zoeckler, *Dilthey und die Hermeneutik* (Stuttgart 1975), a discussion of Dilthey's philosophy from a Marxist point of view.

7 R.A. Makkreel, *Dilthey, Philosopher of the Human Studies* (1975).

8 According to Sauerland the rehabilitation of Dilthey began with K. Müller-Vollmer's *Towards a Phenomenological Theory of Literature: a Study of W. Dilthey's Poetik* (1963). She also quotes Renee Welleck writing in the second volume of his *A History of Modern Criticism*: 'What he has to say is as relevant as it was sixty years ago'.

9 See, for instance, G. Lukacs, *Die Zerstoerung der Vernunft* (1962).

10 See Chapter 11 for a fuller discussion.

11 See, for instance, *The Positivist Dispute in German Sociology*; the original German version of 1969 was translated by G. Adley and D. Frisby (1976).

12 Note particularly J. Habermas, *Knowledge and Human Interest*, trans. J.J. Shapiro (1971).

References

Chapter 3.   Dilthey the man

1 They are at Münster where this work has been done with loving care by Mrs L. Wittel.
2 Professor Gründer of Bochum University has interested himself in this subject and bases some of his knowledge on conversations with Dilthey's daughter Clara.
3 Now published in Volumes XV, XVI and XVII under the title *Contributions to the Nineteenth-century History of Ideas.*
4 Quoted from W. Nohl, 'Wilhelm Dilthey' in *Die Grossen Deutschen*, (1957). I have italicised the part of the letter written in English; the rest is in German.
5 The confusion of tenses is in the original and is, no doubt, due to his agitation.
6 See above Chapter 1, note 9.
7 See above note 4.

Chapter 4.   The philosophy of life

1 From fragments for the rewriting of *Building Blocks for a Poetic* (called the *Poetic* for short).
2 From *Present-day Culture and Philosophy.*
3 From *The Natural System of the Human Studies*, originally published *Archiv* (1892/3).
4 From *System of Ethics* lecture course composed about 1900.
5 From *Historical Consciousness and the World-views.*
6 From *Leibniz and his Age*, originally published *Deutsche Rundschau* (1900).
7 From *Evolutionary Pantheism and its Relation to Older Pantheistic Systems*, originally published *Archiv* (1900).
8 From *A Preface* written in 1911.
9 From Nature of Philosophy (1907).
10 From *Theory of World-views* section on *The Basic Idea of my Philosophy* (1900).

Chapter 5.   The human studies

1 For the circle of knowledge see also pp.119, 129–31 and 159.
2 Particularly in *Ideas about a Descriptive and Analytical Psychology* (Vol. V).

Chapter 6.   Understanding (Verstehen)

1 The most sustained theoretical discussions of understanding are to be found in Vol. VII. Many of these passages have been translated in my *Meaning in History* and in *SW.*
2 See Chapter 11.

Chapter 7.   Expressions

1 Dilthey's most explicit philosophic discussion of expressions comes in the

Drafts towards a Critique of Historical Reason, Vol. VII, pp.205–10, trans. in *SW*, pp.218–25. The references to Dilthey's views on literature come from his aesthetic writings and literary criticism.

2 From *The Eighteenth Century and the Historical World, Deutsche Rundschau* (1900).

3 Quoted by G. Misch in his introduction. See above p.14.

4 From *The Dream*, lecture given on his seventieth birthday.

5 From *A Study of the Foundations of the Human Studies, Proceedings* (1905).

6 The fullest account of Goethe comes in a long essay originally published in 1887 and revised for inclusions in *Experience and Poetry* (1905) (part of it trans. in *SW*). An examination of Goethe's world-view and its influence is contained in a chapter of the Schleiermacher biography (also trans. in *SW*) and a further discussion is to be found in *The Poetical and Philosophic Movement in Germany 1770–1800* (1867), his inaugural lecture at Basel. There are numerous other references to Goethe throughout Dilthey's writings. For example, he discusses Goethe's view of his own life in Vol. VII (p.199), trans. in my *Meaning in History*, p.88.

Chapter 8.   Meaning

1 From *Drafts towards a Critique of Historical Reason*.

2 In *Thinking and Meaning* Ayer wrote that 'to say what a particular sentence means is to give an interpretation of it in terms of other symbols'. Because of the word 'say' this is a harmless tautology, but J.D. Mabbott, reviewing the book in *Mind* (vol. LVII, 1948), comments that 'Ayer refuses to distinguish a thought from an expression and holds that if there is more in an occurrence of thinking than the symbols concerned (i.e. the "understanding" of the "meaning" of these symbols) this can be fully explained as the relation of these symbols to other symbols. But when I say "the meaning dawns on me" I am sure there is something non-linguistic to explain.'

3 From *The Poet's Imagination, Building Blocks for a Poetic* (1887).

4 From fragments for the rewriting of the *Poetic*. Dilthey's use of 'category' is explained below pp.132–6.

5 From a paper *The Construction of the Historical World in the Human Studies* read to the Prussian Academy of Science in 1910 and published in their proceedings.

6 See above note 4.

7 An extensive contemporary debate on this topic can be found in *Modes of Individualism and Collectivism*, ed. J. O'Neill (1973).

8 From *The Function of Anthropology in Sixteenth- and Seventeenth-Century Culture, Proceedings* (1904).

9 From a draft for one of his papers for the Prussian Academy of Science.

10 See above note 3.

Chapter 9.   'The Critique of Historical Reason'

1 From *The Young Hegel* (1905).

References

2 From *The Three Main Forms of Systems in the First Half of the Nineteenth Century, Archiv* (1898).

3 In *Ideas about a Descriptive and Analytical Psychology*, called *The Ideas* for short, Vol. V, p.151 (trans. in *SW*, pp.90–1).

4 From *Theory of World-views* section called *What Philosophy is about* (1880).

5 From *Ideas*, trans. in *SW* p.94.

6 It is formulated in G. Vico, *The New Science* (1774), section 331.

7 From *An Attempt of an Analysis of Moral Consciousness* (1864).

8 Most of Dilthey's discussion of the categories is contained in *Drafts for a Critique of Historical Reason* (Vol. VII, pp.189–220), trans. in *SW*, pp.207–45.

9 From *The Significance of Literary Archives for the Study of the History of Philosophy, Archiv* (1889).

10 From a *Study towards the Foundations of the Human Studies, Proceedings* (1905).

11 From *Contribution to the Solution of the Question about the Origin of our Belief in the Reality of the External World and its Justification* (1890).

12 From *The Possibility of a Universally Valid Pedagogic Science* (1888).

13 From *The Three Epochs of Modern Aesthetics and its Present Task* (1892).

14 From *Historical Consciousness and the World-views*.

Chapter 10. The methodology of the human studies

1 From W. Wordsworth, 'The Tables Turned', line 28.

2 *The Origin of Hermeneutics* (1900) in Vol. V, trans. in *SW*, pp.147–263.

3 In a review (in *Philosophy*, January 1978) of *Explanation*, ed. Stephan Körner (1975), Bambrough is quoted as making exactly the same point: 'To seek the causes of the French Revolution ... is to explore connections and cross-references in complex patterns of particularity in a manner analogous to that involved in the critical analysis of a novel or a symphony or a classical work of architecture or painting or philosophy.'

4 From *Ideas*.

5 From *The Young Hegel*.

6 See below Chapter 11.

7 From discarded versions of his papers to the Prussian Academy.

8 From *The Young Hegel*.

9 M. Mead, *Sex and Temperament in Three Primitive Societies*.

10 From fragments for supplementing *The Young Hegel*.

11 from *Historical Consciousness and the World-views*.

12 See above Chapter 9, note 11.

13 From a *Study of the Foundations of the Human Studies, Proceedings* (1905).

14 Dilthey's conception found particularly lucid expression in Lakatos' remark 'Philosophy of science without history of science is empty; history of science without philosophy of science is blind'. I have no idea if this was due to Dilthey's direct influence or if Lakatos had reached independently the conclusion drawn by Dilthey a hundred years earlier.

Chapter 11. Dilthey's influence

1 *Logische Untersuchungen* appeared originally in 1901. A translation of it by J.N. Findlay (*Logical Investigations*) came out in 1970. *Ideen zu einer reinen Phaenomenologie* first appeared in 1913 and was translated by W.R. Boyce Gibson (*Ideas: General Introduction to Pure Phenomenology*) in 1931.

2 See *Die Krisis der Europaeischen Wissenschaften und die transcendentale Phenomenologie* (1936), trans. D. Carr, *The Crisis of European Sciences and Transcendental Phenomenology* (1970).

3 For example, Maurice Natanson who wrote *Phenomenology, Role and Reason* Springfield (1974) and edited *Phenomenology and the Social Sciences* (1973).

4 See, for instance, M. Roche, *Phenomenology, Language and the Social Sciences* (1973).

5 See, for example, H. Garfinkel, *Studies in Ethnomethodology* (1967).

6 See, for instance, M. Scheler, *Die Stellung des Menschen in Kosmos* (1928), and H. Plessner, Die Stufen des Organischen der Mensch (1928) and *Zwischen Philosophie und Gesellschaft* (1953).

7 R.G. Collingwood (1889–1943), English philosopher and historian. B. Croce (1866–1952), outstanding modern Italian philosopher.

8 See above p.147.

9 See R.E. Palmer, *Hermeneutics: Interpretation Theory in Schleiermacher, Dilthey, Heidegger and Gadamer* (1969).

10 *The Fontana Dictionary of Modern Thought*, ed. A. Bullock and O. Stalybrass.

11 For a history and bibliography of the Frankfurt school, see M. Jay *The Dialectical Imagination* (1973).

12 J. Ortega y Gasset (1883–1955), distinguished Spanish philosopher.

13 See E. Spranger *Lebensformen, geisteswissenschaftliche Psychologie und Ethnik ther Persoenlichkeit* (1914).

14 T.W. Adorno and others, *The Authoritarian Personality* (1950).

15 This quotation is specifically about Adorno's research on radio-listening and comes from *Scientific Experiences of an European Scholar in America*.

16 See several references in W.G. Runciman, *A Critique of Max Weber's Philosophy of Social Science* (1972).

17 See A. Dawe, 'The Relevance of Values', and R. Moore, 'History, Economics and Religion', papers reproduced in A. Sahay's *Max Weber and Modern Sociology* (1971).

18 L. Landgrebe, *Philosophie der Gegenwart* (1952), p.109.

19 From his 'The Humanistic Challenge to Sociology' in *Humanistic Society: Today's Challenge to Sociology*, ed. J.F. Glass and J.R. Staude (1972). The quotations from works by Matson, Turner, Gouldner and Wrong which follow are also taken from this volume.

20 Floyd Matson, 'The Human Image: "Science and the Understanding of Man"' in *The Broken Image* (1964).

References

21 From A. Ryan's introduction (p.6) to *The Philosophy of Social Explanation*, (1973), which he edited.

22 From 'Towards a Reflexive Sociology' in *The Coming Crisis of Western Sociology* (1970).

23 From 'The Borrowed Toolbox and Conservative Man' in *Radical Man* (1970).

24 From *The Human Sciences and Philosophy* (1966), trans. 1969.

25 From 'The Oversocialised Conception of Man in Modern Sociology', *American Social Review* (1961).

26 From 'Introduction to the Sociology of Industry' in *Society: Problems and Methods of Study*, ed. A.T. Welford (1962).

Index to quotations from Dilthey

General index

Page numbers in italic refer to main entries

General Index

Nature of Philosophy, The, 43, 60
Naturwissenschaften, 59
Neo-Marxism, 16, 17, 18f, 168f, 178
Niebuhr, 123
Nietzsche, 2, 42
Norms, 64, 107

Objective idealism, 49

Part-whole, 34, 119f, 176; *see also under*
  Categories
Phenomenology, vii, 167
Personality, 121, 151f, 171
Philology, 10, 123
Philosophy, vii, 2f, 10, 61f, 67, 71, 128,
  161; of human studies, 164; of language,
  57; of life, 110; of science, 17, 18, 50
Physiology, 26, 158
Plessner, 139
Poetry and Experience, 13
Politics, 20, 25, 62, 67
Positivism, 20, 49, 53, 79, 147, 169
Power, *see under* Categories
Practical disciplines, 70
Pragmatism, 144
Principles, 64, 66
Psychoanalysis, 165
Psychology, vii, 20, 56, 58; as part of the
  Geisteswissenschaften, 62, 67; critique
  of, 50; descriptive, 14; Dilthey's influ-
  ence on, *169–72*; Dilthey's interest in,
  12; Dilthey's writings on, 14; history
  and, 10, 68, 69, 72, 159f; literature and,
  164; material of, 102; phenomenology
  and, 167; physiology and, 158; sociology
  and, 71, 153, 158; usefulness to other
  disciplines, 11, 102
Purpose, 63f, 65f, 90, 121; in history, 155;
  of literary criticism, 107

Ranke, 123
Reason, 3, 107, 124, 179
Reflection, 45
Relativity, relativism, 48, 49f, *141–2*, 164
Rules, 64

Sartre, 16
Scheler, 139
Schelling, 49, 51
Schlegel, 51

Schleiermacher, biography of, 13, 17, 30f,
  32f, 39, 41, 121; Dilthey's work on his
  hermeneutics, 14, 26; Dilthey's work on
  his letters, 26; his concept of hermeneutics, 148; Spinoza's influence on, 51
Self-knowledge, 45, 52, 56, 177
Social sciences, 18, 46, 67
Sociology, vii, 20, 58, 70; Dilthey's influ-
  ence on, *172–6*; history and, 68, 164;
  literature and, 164; methods of, 85; part
  of the *Geisteswissenschaften*, 62, 67;
  phenomenology and, 117; psychology
  and, 71, 153, 158; Weber's sociology,
  110
Spengler, 168
Spinoza, 49, 51
Spranger, 31, 34, 63, 79, 166, 171
*Study of the History of the Disciplines
  dealing with Man, Society and the State,
  The*, 37, 143
Style, 93
Sympathy, 75
Systematic human disciplines, 67f
Systematic human studies, 20
Systems, 70, 118, 144

Temporality, 133
Theology, 9
Theoretical disciplines, 70
Theory of knowledge, *see* Epistemology
Toynbee, 165
Troeltsch, 173
Typologies, 173
Typology of World-Views, 43

Understanding, *74–87*, 147; made possible
  by experience, 139; of actions 91; of
  literary works, 106; of meaning, 121;
  presuppositions of, 127, 131; principles
  of, 132f; purpose and, 64; Weber's concept of, 173
Unity, 9

Values, 64–5, 107, 161, 176f

Weber, vii, 1, 110, 165, 166, 173
Weltanschauung, 47f; *see also Typology of
  World-Views*
Wittgenstein, 17

Zusammenhang, 9

197